Y0-CAV-418

INVITATION TO
THE NEW TESTAMENT EPISTLES III

This volume continues a series of commentaries on the books of the Bible, specially designed to answer the need for a lively, contemporary guide to the written Word. Here is the best of contemporary biblical scholarship, together with the world-renowned *Jerusalem Bible* text. In addition, there are study questions that will provoke and inspire further discussion.

The Pauline Epistles have traditionally been considered as letters from the great Apostle to the Gentiles to the churches he founded or to his trusted co-workers. They serve to warn of trouble, to correct problems, to instruct in the faith, to refresh a troubled or flagging spirit—in short, to remind the Church of the reality of God in their lives.

The church of the Colossians was founded in an area that tended toward exotic, cultic forms of religion. Paul must convince these newly baptized Christians that it is only in the Church of Jesus Christ that salvation can be found.

In the Epistle to the Ephesians, the writer exhorts his hearers to remember that the Church is the place where God's will is revealed to humans, a place of unity founded by God to reconcile Jews and Gentiles to himself and therefore to each other.

The Pastoral Epistles—1 and 2 Timothy and Titus—are personal letters from Paul to his closest co-workers who are collaborators in Paul's mission. He uses these letters to teach his associates how to be preachers, teachers and administrators—how to lead the churches they have founded. Paul refreshes their spirits by recalling to their minds the basis of their ministries, the love of God and Jesus.

Just as he spoke to the Christians of his day, Paul speaks to today's followers of Christ. The problems he wrote about are still found in today's world and studying these Epistles can be of help, solace and inspiration.

INVITATION TO THE NEW TESTAMENT EPISTLES III presents these Epistles and their message in a format that can be easily used for individual study, daily meditation and/or group discussion. It is an indispensable volume for any Christian library.

INVITATION TO
THE NEW TESTAMENT EPISTLES III

INVITATION TO THE NEW TESTAMENT EPISTLES III

A Commentary on Colossians, Ephesians, 1 Timothy, 2 Timothy and Titus with Complete Text from The Jerusalem Bible

LUKE TIMOTHY JOHNSON

IMAGE BOOKS
A Division of Doubleday & Company, Inc.
Garden City, New York
1980

The text of the Epistles to the Colossians, the Ephesians, 1 Timothy, 2 Timothy and Titus is from The Jerusalem Bible, copyright © 1966 by Darton, Longman & Todd, Ltd., and Doubleday & Company, Inc. Used by permission of the publisher.

ISBN: 0-385-14798-8
Library of Congress Catalog Card Number: 79-7787

Commentary Copyright © 1980 by Luke Timothy Johnson
General Introduction Copyright © 1977 by Robert J. Karris
All Rights Reserved
Printed in the United States of America
First Edition

CONTENTS

CONTENTS

ABBREVIATIONS OF THE BOOKS
OF THE BIBLE

Ac	Acts	Lk	Luke
Am	Amos	Lm	Lamentations
Ba	Baruch	Lv	Leviticus
1 Ch	1 Chronicles	1 M	1 Maccabees
2 Ch	2 Chronicles	2 M	2 Maccabees
1 Co	1 Corinthians	Mi	Micah
2 Co	2 Corinthians	Mk	Mark
Col	Colossians	Ml	Malachi
Dn	Daniel	Mt	Matthew
Dt	Deuteronomy	Na	Nahum
Ep	Ephesians	Nb	Numbers
Est	Esther	Ne	Nehemiah
Ex	Exodus	Ob	Obadiah
Ezk	Ezekiel	1 P	1 Peter
Ezr	Ezra	2 P	2 Peter
Ga	Galatians	Ph	Philippians
Gn	Genesis	Phm	Philemon
Hab	Habakkuk	Pr	Proverbs
Heb	Hebrews	Ps	Psalms
Hg	Haggai	Qo	Ecclesiastes
Ho	Hosea	Rm	Romans
Is	Isaiah	Rt	Ruth
Jb	Job	Rv	Revelation
Jdt	Judith	1 S	1 Samuel
Jg	Judges	2 S	2 Samuel
Jl	Joel	Sg	Song of Songs
Jm	James	Si	Ecclesiasticus
Jn	John	Tb	Tobit
1 Jn	1 John	1 Th	1 Thessalonians
2 Jn	2 John	2 Th	2 Thessalonians
3 Jn	3 John	1 Tm	1 Timothy
Jon	Jonah	2 Tm	2 Timothy
Jos	Joshua	Tt	Titus
Jr	Jeremiah	Ws	Wisdom
Jude	Jude	Zc	Zechariah
1 K	1 Kings	Zp	Zephaniah
2 K	2 Kings		

ABBREVIATIONS OF THE BOOKS OF THE BIBLE

GENERAL INTRODUCTION TO
THE DOUBLEDAY NEW TESTAMENT
COMMENTARY SERIES

Let me introduce this new commentary series on the New Testament by sharing some experiences. In my job as New Testament Book Review Editor for the *Catholic Biblical Quarterly,* scores of books pass through my hands each year. As I evaluate these books and send them out to reviewers, I cannot help but think that so little of this scholarly research will make its way into the hands of the educated lay person.

In talking at biblical institutes and to charismatic and lay study groups, I find an almost unquenchable thirst for the Word of God. People want to learn more; they want to study. But when they ask me to recommend commentaries on the New Testament, I'm stumped. What commentaries can I put into their hands, commentaries that do not have the technical jargon of scholars and that really communicate to the educated laity?

The goal of this popular commentary series is to make the best of contemporary scholarship available to the educated lay person in a highly readable and understandable way. The commentaries avoid footnotes and other scholarly apparatus. They are short and sweet. The authors make their points in a clear way and don't fatigue their readers with unnecessary detail.

Another outstanding feature of this commentary series is that it is based on The Jerusalem Bible translation, which is serialized with the commentary. This lively and easily understandable translation has received rave reviews from millions of readers. It is the interstate of translations and avoids the stoplights of local-road translations.

A signal feature of the commentaries on the Gospels is that they explore the way each evangelist used the sayings and deeds of Jesus to meet the needs of his church. The commentators answer the question: How did each evangelist guide, challenge, teach, and console the members of his community with the message of Jesus? The commentators are not interested in the evangelist's message for its own sake, but explain that message with one eye on present application.

This last-mentioned feature goes hand and glove with the innovative feature of appending Study Questions to the explanations of individual passages. By means of these Study Questions the commentator moves from an explanation of the message of the evangelist to a consideration of how this message might apply to believers today.

Each commentator has two highly important qualifications: scholarly expertise and the proven ability to communicate the results of solid scholarship to the people of God.

I am confident that this new commentary series will

meet a real need as it helps people to unlock a door to the storehouse of God's Word where they will find food for life.

ROBERT J. KARRIS, O.F.M.
Associate Professor of New Testament Studies,
Catholic Theological Union and
Chicago Cluster of Theological Schools

INTRODUCTION

All the letters you will be reading in this book come from the Apostle Paul. Precisely how they come from him is disputed. They all claim (by way of their greetings) to be from Paul, and the tradition of the Church from earliest times has affirmed that they all were written by him. Yet, many scholars of the New Testament have wondered whether this traditional attribution is correct, and a debate over the authenticity of these letters has gone on for well over a hundred years. If a poll were to be taken from among those qualified in these matters, many would say that Colossians was written by Paul; but fewer would be willing to say Ephesians was, and fewer still would want to put down their names in support of the authenticity of the Pastorals (i.e. 1, 2 Timothy, Titus).

REASONS FOR QUESTIONING
PAULINE AUTHORSHIP

There are good reasons why doubts, and serious
ones, have arisen concerning the Pauline authorship of
these letters. The placement of them within Paul's career, the style of the Greek language (especially vocab-
ulary and sentence structure), the theological perspec-
tives, the kinds of heretics and the way they are
rebutted, the use of the Old Testament and of traditional community teaching, the church structure en-
visaged; all these factors, some more than others, come
into play when a decision is reached whether the same
man who wrote Romans and 1 Corinthians could also
have written Ephesians and 2 Timothy.

For some observers, the differences in each of these
areas seem so great as to deny the possibility of Paul
being at work. For others, the differences (though ac-
knowledged as real) are seen as less significant than
the elements of continuity.

AN IMPORTANT QUALIFICATION

It should be pointed out at once that the debate over
authorship and dating is not one whose resolution decides the value of these letters. The documents of the
New Testament have enduring validity and significance
for the Church, not because they were written by this
person or that, but because the Holy Spirit has enabled
the Church to discern which of the many writings

emerging from primitive Christianity truly reflected its
self-understanding, and possessed the power to renew
the Church's life through history; which writings, in
short, revealed to people God's Word in human dic-
tion. These were collected in the Church's canon of
Scripture, her working bibliography of faith, as the enduring norm of Christian existence in the world. These
letters, then, are looked to by Christians, not because
they were written by Paul (for that would amount to a
cult of personality), but because they ultimately derive
from the Holy Spirit who spoke through witnesses as
diverse then as now.

ONE WAY OF UNDERSTANDING
PAULINE ORIGIN

The scholars who reject Pauline authorship of these
letters tend to have a very sharp image of the historical
figure Paul and his teaching. It is the Paul of Galatians
and 1 Corinthians, the fiery defender of God's grace
and human freedom. It is the Apostle who debates,
refutes and cajoles with great passion, compelled as he
is by the urgency of his distinctive call from God; a
figure sometimes heroic, frequently complex, but never
boring. His vision of the Church, they say, is colored
by his expectation of the end of the world. His communities are filled with the Holy Spirit and have but little organization, as they await the coming of the Lord.
He gives scant attention to community organization or
ethics, for he sees the Church as an interim community
rapidly approaching its end.

It is hard to fit this picture of Paul to the calm and

equable tone of Ephesians and the Pastorals, with their placidity and piety, and with their emphasis on the Church, less as an eschatological community than as God's household, which, to all appearances, has settled in for a longer wait than Paul would have suspected.

The lack of edge in these letters leads some students to conclude that they were written after the death of Paul by his followers, in his name and authority. No deception was intended by attaching Paul's name to these writings, for pseudonymity was an accepted literary convention of the age. Actually, the Pastorals on the one hand, and Colossians/Ephesians on the other, are so different even from each other that there is thought to be two streams of Pauline tradition at work: one of a more speculative bent (Col/Ep), the other of a more practical (the Pastorals). Why were they written? For the same reasons Paul's genuine letters were: to strengthen communities in their faith, and to preserve the authentic Pauline Gospel in the face of attacks. By whom? Anonymous students of Paul who passed on his teaching in new circumstances, but who (with the possible exception of the author of Ephesians) did not measure up to their master's originality. When? No one knows, but there are many guesses: anywhere from shortly after Paul's death (Col/Ep) to the middle of the second century (the Pastorals).

In this understanding, these letters can be considered "Pauline" in the broad sense, for they clearly align themselves with the Apostle, and (even the Pastorals) contain authentic aspects of Paul's distinctive teaching. But they should be read by the discerning reader as a witness, not to the life of Paul and his teaching, but to a second-generation Christianity, in which the attempt to preserve Paul's thought was inevitably affected by dramatically changed circumstances: the Lord had not come in the way expected, and the mission to the Jews had failed, resulting in a Church consisting far more in Gentiles than in Jews.

ANOTHER VIEW OF PAULINE AUTHORSHIP

Although the position just sketched represents a majority opinion among contemporary New Testament scholars, there is much to be said for the Pauline authorship of these letters in a more direct sense, simply on historical grounds. For those who find this position attractive (and the present writer is among them), the figure of Paul and the shape of the primitive Church are equally important, but differently construed.

They point out that even the Paul of the undoubtedly genuine letters is a writer of many facets, showing as many sides of himself as there are letters from him still in our possession. They suggest that there is great difficulty in deriving a totally consistent "Pauline teaching" on any given doctrine or practice, and that the teaching we find in these disputed letters is well within his range. They remind us that Paul was more than a wandering preacher. He was also the founder of churches and a consummate organizer, a man who stood at the head of a vast missionary enterprise, with many co-workers and associates with whom he was in frequent contact. Although a creative theologian, Paul saw himself as a man of tradition. Although eager to promote the gifts of the Spirit, he dealt firmly with any disorderliness in his communities.

As for the issue of the Greek style, which looms so large in this discussion, these scholars point to two factors which make that issue less than determinative. First, ancient rhetorical ideals stressed great variety in expression; a good writer was one who could adapt his language to the demands of the occasion and the proper literary forms. Style was regarded less as an expression of the inner personality than as a vehicle of persuasion. Second, there is the strong possibility that Paul followed the custom of dictating his letters to a secretary, and they were frequently given considerable freedom in composition. For all their occasional nature, Paul's letters were not dashed off in a rush. The careful argumentation of his letters suggests the development of ideas within the context of a group of students.

That Paul had associates of ability is clear. That they should be considered a "Pauline school" is appropriate. But it is possible to see these associates at work in the shaping of Paul's correspondence under his direction and during his lifetime. This view of Pauline authorship is not without problems. But it makes possible an intelligent reading of the letters without excessive appeal to historical reconstructions which are more speculative than solid.

THE PERSPECTIVE OF THIS COMMENTARY

The debate over authenticity (which, it must be emphasized, is a genial one among persons equally dedicated to the truth) has unfortunately tended to obscure the richness of these letters. Although this commentary is written from the point of view of Pauline authorship in the direct sense, that is not its point. Rather, each letter is read for the purpose of discovering its distinctive witness to the mystery of God in Christ. You will find the letters here in a different order than in your Bible; this arrangement allows for a clearer presentation of each document. A short introduction to each letter touches on the probable occasion and purpose for writing, and the letter's major emphasis. The commentary on individual passages seeks to elucidate the argument of the author, and provide helpful information about, or insights into obscurities. Whether from Paul or not, these letters are part of that body of writings in which, we confess, the Word of God speaks to the Church and the heart of every individual. Allowing this Word to speak is the goal of every responsible interpretation.

The reader of this book would do well to have a copy of the whole Bible in hand. Many references have been made to other Pauline writings, as well as to other parts of Scripture. These provide the best commentary on the text. The words of the Scripture, and not those of the interpreter, should rivet the reader's attention. Each passage should be read first, preferably aloud, and reflected upon. The reading of the comments should be followed by a return to the Scripture. The study questions at the end of each section may help stimulate this process of reading, reflecting and rereading.

From time to time, it has been thought necessary to offer another translation of the Greek text than that given by *The Jerusalem Bible*. This should not be

taken as a criticism of that translation, which is in
many respects admirable. But in some instances, a rendering closer to the literal meaning of the Greek helps
the reader grasp the argument.

ACKNOWLEDGMENTS

The author of this small commentary enjoyed an un-
usual number of willing and helpful listeners, whose
perceptive reactions helped shape this book. Among
them, he must give special thanks to Carl Holladay,
Abraham Malherbe, and John Fitzgerald. David Drake
gave careful attention to the accuracy of the references
and to the spelling. For the love and support of his
wife, Joy, to whom this book is dedicated, the author
can give no adequate expression of thanks.

LUKE TIMOTHY JOHNSON
Yale Divinity School
New Haven, Connecticut
April 30, 1979

INVITATION TO
THE NEW TESTAMENT EPISTLES III

The Letter to the Colossian Church
Christ, The Measure of Christian Maturity

While he was imprisoned (4:3,10,18), Paul wrote this letter to the Christians of a small town of Phrygia. This was a part of the Roman Province of Asia Minor which, as ancient sources indicate, was particularly given to exotic forms of religiosity. Mystery, magic, and prophecy of every sort seemed to flourish in its cities and mountain towns alike.

For those who had recently become Christians, as for their neighbors, Christianity must have appeared as one more cult in an already highly competitive situation. Comparison was inevitable, and as usual, odious. Wherever there is more than one claim to ultimate sufficiency (and this is what is involved when a cult promises salvation to its adherents), there is bound to be a certain amount of threat to the holders of any one claim. The threat comes not only from without, but from within. If others are saying that their way is better, more powerful; if they have extraordinary visions to back up their claims and we do not; if they can point

to an antiquity of law and observance and we cannot;
how solid in fact is our claim? What is the basis of our
hope, and how reliable?

These questions become more pressing when the
founder of the cult community has gone away, and is,
in fact, imprisoned. Faced with this, we grow less sure
of the sufficiency of his teaching. Perhaps we should
pay attention to those, even within the fellowship, who
insinuate that our belief in Christ, while a beginning, is
not adequate if we wish to reach perfection, become
truly mature; that observance of ascetic rules and mys-
tical experiences are required if we are to reach our full
growth in salvation.

Epaphras, the founder of the Colossian community
(1:7, 4:12) was imprisoned with Paul, and shared
with him not only his joy in the flourishing Church he
had established at Paul's direction, but also his concern
for the community's steadfastness in the face of this in-
cipient crisis of identity.

When Paul sent the runaway slave, Onesimus, back
to his master, Philemon (cf. Phm 11–12, Col 4:9), he
used the occasion to compose, together with Timothy
(1:1), this letter of support to the Colossian church
and its sister communities of Laodicea and Hierapolis,
which also were under the care of Epaphras (4:13).
To further strengthen these communities in their commitment, Paul sent along Tychicus, one of his most
trusted delegates (4:7; cf. Ac 20:4, Ep 6:21, 2 Tm
4:12, Tt 3:12) to "give you news about us and to reassure you."

The difficulties faced by the Colossians are not
unlike those confronted by the Galatians, a church
Paul himself had founded. There too, teachers had

come among the believers claiming that belief in
Christ was not sufficient, that to be saved one needed
also to follow the Law of Moses and observe special
feasts (Ga 1:6, 3:1–2, 4:8–11, 5:1–4). There, as here,
Paul argues that the saving work of Jesus Christ is the
beginning and end of the Christian Gospel; that to seek
a further righteousness, a perfection based on observance of law, ritual, or mystic initiation, is in reality an
apostasy.

In Galatians, Paul was speaking to his own community, and the incursion of false teachers was actual and
powerful; therefore, his polemic was sharp, and his argumentation based on the claims of his opponents. In
Colossians, the danger appears not to be so extreme,
and Paul's attack is muted; gentler, too, because this
community did not know him as its founder. Paul's argument here is carried less by the interpretation of the
Scripture, than by reference to the liturgical (especially
baptismal) traditions shared by all early Christians,
and intelligible to these newly converted pagans whose
commitment to Christ was being tested by the offer of
more seductive mysteries than those to be found in the
cult of a crucified messiah.

The threat to the Colossians happened long ago.
Hearing only Paul's version of the threat, we are forced
to pick up clues here and there from the text, if we
wish to piece together the claims of the opposition. But
the issue faced by the Colossians is an enduring one for
all Christians: what is the basis of the Christian hope,
and in what does Christian maturity consist? Does our
hope stem from what we achieve? And does maturity
consist in adding observance of rules and mysticism
unto grace? Or does it consist in an ever deeper insight

into the gift given us in Christ, an insight which leads perhaps not to ecstasy, but to self-emptying service and love for the community?

This issue dominates Colossians, but does not exhaust its continuing significance. In encouraging the Colossians to a deeper insight into the Mystery of Christ, Paul shared with them and us his own perception of Christ's nature and work which is cosmic in scope and immediate in pertinence: our hope in Christ is not foolish, for a hope based in Him is based in what is most real: the presence and power of God.

Colossians 1:1–12
THE GIFT GROWS WITH THANKSGIVING

¹ From Paul, appointed by God to be apostle of Christ Jesus, and from our brother Timothy ² to the saints in Colossae, our faithful brothers in Christ: Grace and peace to you from God our Father.

³ We have never failed to remember you in our prayers and to give thanks for you to God, the ⁴ Father of our Lord Jesus Christ, ·ever since we heard about your faith in Christ Jesus and the ⁵ love that you show toward all the saints ·because of the hope which is stored up for you in heaven. It is only recently that you heard of this, when it was announced in the message of the truth. The ⁶ Good News ·which has reached you is spreading all over the world and producing the same results as it has among you ever since the day when you heard about God's grace and understood what ⁷ this really is. ·Epaphras, who taught you, is one of our closest fellow workers and a faithful dep- ⁸ uty for us as Christ's servant, ·and it was he who told us all about your love in the Spirit.

⁹ That will explain why, ever since the day he told us, we have never failed to pray for you, and

what we ask God is that through perfect wisdom
and spiritual understanding you should reach the
10 fullest knowledge of his will. ·So you will be able
to lead the kind of life which the Lord expects of
you, a life acceptable to him in all its aspects;
showing the results in all the good actions you do
11 and increasing your knowledge of God. ·You
will have in you the strength, based on his own
glorious power, never to give in, but to bear any-
12 thing joyfully, ·thanking the Father who has made
it possible for you to join the saints and with them
to inherit the light.

✠

The thanksgiving and prayer (1:3–12) which follow
the characteristic Pauline greeting (1:1–2) express
something of Paul's deepest conviction about life, and
are of real importance for the understanding of this
letter.

Paul sees all of life, indeed all that exists, as a gift
coming from the God who is Father, and sees that the
most properly human response to life is thanksgiving.
This perception of reality makes all the difference. It
affects the way we see ourselves and the world. If
human existence is the whim of a faceless fate, then
human worth is dependent on what men and women
can achieve for themselves, and their perfection will
consist in the sum of their achievements. But if abso-
lutely all being and worth comes from the hand of a
loving creator by gift, then maturity and perfection are
to be found in the growing acceptance of God's une-

quivocal acceptance. So, as Paul's life is one of constant thanksgiving, he wishes the Colossians to always give thanks (1:12, 2:6–7, 3:16–17, 4:2). The more the Giver is thanked, the more real the gift grows in the minds and hearts of those who praise.

The thanksgiving and prayer also allow Paul to touch lightly on the concerns he will develop later in the letter. His pastoral touch is sensitive and sure. He thanks God because the Colossians, since the day they heard the Gospel, have demonstrated in their lives the classic Christian expressions of response: faith in God (1:2,4) and love toward the brothers and sisters (1:4,8). They have done this because of their hope, 1:5. (For this triad elsewhere in Paul, cf. 1 Th 1:3, 1 Co 13:13).

They have responded to God by hearing "the message of truth." This characterization of the Gospel (cf. also Ep 1:13, 2 Tm 2:15, Jm 1:18, 1 P 1:22) is not accidental. The Good News heard by the Colossians revealed to them the truth about God's way with the world: that whatever the fearsome potency of pretender gods, his is the ultimate power, shown to be, in the work of Christ, a power of love to save. Because of this truth, the "hope stored up for you in heaven" (1:5), even though it is not seen, is sure, for God is true.

Paul acknowledges that this message has taken root among them and, as throughout the world, is "bearing fruit and growing" (the *JB* translation here [1:6] obscures the Greek). The use of this phrase hints at Paul's concern, for immediately in his prayer (1:10) and again later in the letter (4:12), he will express the desire that the Colossians grow and bear fruit, that is, reach maturity as Christians. This maturity will enable them to live in a manner pleasing to God (1:10).

But what is the way to this maturity? Is it some additional teaching or practice beyond what they already have? No. They are to hold to the word of truth "just as they learned it from Epaphras" (1:7, with a different emphasis in *JB*). What is required for their further growth is a deepened *insight* into what they have already been given, a "perfect wisdom and spiritual understanding" (1:9). With this, they will learn more profoundly what the gift (grace) of God "really is" (1:6), and enter more deeply into this grace the more fully they appreciate its power among and within them. With this maturity, they will be able to endure anything joyfully (1:11), even the subtle pressures from those seeking to suborn them; the result will be still more thanksgiving toward him who has given them this inexpressible gift.

The last verse of the prayer forms a transition to the next part of the letter, in which Paul spells out for the Colossians the dimensions of this gift. It is God who is at work among them: he has qualified them to share in the inheritance of the saints (i.e. other Christians), a possession so fundamental and all-encompassing Paul characterizes it by one of the most primitive and powerful of religious symbols, the light. Paul uses a stronger word in 1:12 than the *JB*'s "made it possible" suggests. Literally, he says God has "qualified them." Later, Paul will urge, "let no one disqualify you" (2:18), and here is the reason: God has already qualified them, already made them acceptable to him by gift.

STUDY QUESTION: The way we pray shows how we believe. What is said about our faith if the prayer of petition is the only kind we use?

Colossians 1:13–23
THE DIMENSIONS OF THE GIFT

13 Because that is what he has done: he has taken us out of the power of darkness and created a place for us in the kingdom of the Son that he
14 loves, ·and in him, we gain our freedom, the forgiveness of our sins.

15 He is the image of the unseen God
and the first-born of all creation,
16 for in him were created
all things in heaven and on earth:
everything visible and everything invisible,
Thrones, Dominations, Sovereignties, Powers—
all things were created through him and for him.
17 Before anything was created, he existed,
and he holds all things in unity.
18 Now the Church is his body,
he is its head.

As he is the Beginning,
he was first to be born from the dead,
so that he should be first in every way;
19 because God wanted all perfection
to be found in him

20   and all things to be reconciled through him
         and for him,
      everything in heaven and everything on earth,
      when he made peace
      by his death on the cross.

21   Not long ago, you were foreigners and en-
      emies, in the way that you used to think and the
22   evil things that you did; ·but now he has recon-
      ciled you, by his death and in that mortal body.
      Now you are able to appear before him holy,
23   pure and blameless—·as long as you persevere
      and stand firm on the solid base of the faith,
      never letting yourselves drift away from the hope
      promised by the Good News, which you have
      heard, which has been preached to the whole
      human race, and of which I, Paul, have become
      the servant.

✠

In order to help the Colossians gain greater insight
into the gift given them by God, Paul shares with them
his own "spiritual understanding" of Christ. He wants
them to see that their whole lives have been changed at
the most radical level because of Christ's work, which
is also (and this is an essential part of his argument)
God's work.

There has been a real change. When they were pagans, they were alienated from God, even his "enemies" (1:21). Is this because God did not love them?
No, it is because they had allowed themselves to be
enslaved by another power, which Paul calls "darkness" (1:13). This enslavement was not external,
alone; there was a darkness in their minds as well

(1:21) and it showed itself in their evil deeds. The picture Paul draws of pagan life resembles that in Rm 1:18-32, and we can profitably refer to that fuller development to understand what is stated only briefly here.

What is the nature of their enslavement? It is a state of alienation from the true God which results from refusing to acknowledge his claim on human existence, and choosing to serve as ultimate other powers in the world, which have no ultimate power but pretend to, that is, idols. Idolatry is not a quaint notion of benighted ancients; it is an endemic disease of the human spirit. When we refuse to accept our lives as gift from the Creator, we seek to establish our own worth, and end up worshiping the works of our hands: our pleasure, possessions, powers.

From this fundamental lie about the world stem all other distortions, even of those spiritual forces created by God to serve humans: the angels. For those estranged from God by idolatry, angels appear as dark and threatening presences, requiring recognition and appeasement if human life is to be secure. It would be condescending to dismiss this perception as naïve. In spite of all our technology, we glimpse, from time to time, a frightening spiritual force for evil in our world, too; a force which goes beyond the vice of individuals, and appears as an atmosphere of evil. We need only think of racism, child pornography, organized crime. But having learned from the word of truth that there is but one ultimate power in the world, and that for good, we have come to see that these forces gain their evil hold only by the service paid them. They are idols which depend on human sacrifice to be real.

And the Colossians, by accepting into their lives the word of truth, have been freed from this enslavement to falsehood. God has transferred them from the kingdom of darkness into the kingdom of light, ruled by his son (1:12–13). They were captives who needed ransoming (1:14), and have now been given the most fundamental of freedoms: freedom from sin and the compulsion of idolatry (1:14); they, who were estranged, have been "reconciled" to God, placed in a state of peace with him (1:20).

How has this astonishing change in their fortunes been accomplished? By the death of Jesus: "he made peace by his death on the cross." The Greek is more elliptical still: "by the blood of his cross." Paul is here using the imagery of covenant. When God makes covenant with humans (that is, establishes peace between them and himself) it is effected and signified by sacrificial blood (cf. Ex 24:3–8, Heb 9:11–14, 1 P 1:2). For Paul, "the cross" is shorthand for Jesus' whole life of obediential faith toward his Father and self-emptying love toward people, which reached its paradoxical climax at his death: "He sacrificed himself for our sins" (Gal 1:4). The obediential death of Jesus (Ph 2:8) is that self-emptying which brings fullness to humans, and places them in a new relationship with God.

But can the death of a man, however virtuous, achieve this reconciliation? If we believe in Christ, how do we know our hope in him is not misplaced, futile? Can full salvation come from any but God? Of course not. And this is precisely the key to Paul's argument in 1:15–20. The power at work in Jesus was not human alone, but the power of God.

To express this, Paul employs a hymn to Christ

(1:15–20) which was probably already known by the Colossians, and may have been used in their liturgy. In its rhythmic structure, it resembles other fragments of traditional hymns directed to Christ found in the New Testament (e.g. 1 Tm 3:16, Ph 2:6–11, 1 P 2:22–24). The understanding of Christ's nature and work, here, closely resembles the prologue to John's Gospel (Jn 1:1–18) and the Letter to the Hebrews (Heb 1:1–3), and elaborates an aspect of Paul's perception of Jesus glimpsed only in passing elsewhere in his letters (e.g. 1 Co 8:6, Ph 2:6–11).

The first Christians knew that the power at work in Jesus, a power they had experienced by receiving his Spirit, went beyond the human and somehow partook of the divine. But how could they express that coming in contact with Jesus was coming in contact with the ultimate power of God, and still maintain their conviction that this power was but One? They turned to the Old Testament writings which had spoken of God's Word and Wisdom as that aspect of God through which he created and sustained the world and brought men to knowledge of himself (cf. Pr 8:22–31, Ws 7:21 – 8:1), and found there an imagery for expressing the ultimate significance of him whom they had come to recognize as "the power and wisdom of God" (1 Co 1:24).

So Paul here speaks of Jesus as being "first" in every respect. In the order of creation, he was first, for he was God's agent in creating all things. Those angelic powers some regard as ultimate? They are but his creatures! As his is the power which sustains the universe (1:17), so his is the power present in the body which is his Church (1:18). He is the first also in the order of

salvation (1:18): his resurrection is the effective sign
that God's power was present to save in his death, and
is the pledge that we too shall be raised by that same
power, for he was raised as a "first-born." The key
phrase is found in 1:19: "God wanted all perfection
(Greek: 'fullness') to be found in him." This phrase is
picked up again at a critical point in Paul's argument
later in the letter, and the implication of it is twofold.
Since Christ, in his very being, carries the image and
power of God, then his work is effectively the work of
God, and the reconciliation of humans is real and complete. And if this is true, then those who believe in him
need not seek for *more* beyond Christ for perfection,
but only grow more deeply into the fullness already
granted them. Their hope is secure.

And this is the point driven home by Paul. They
have been made acceptable to God by the work of
Christ (1:22); the condition of their further growth is
that they build on the foundation given them. Paul uses
explicit architectural imagery in 1:23. They are to
"stand firm on the solid base" as upon the deep foundations of a well-constructed building, and not to "drift
away" after the specious hope offered by other teachings. They *can* stand fast, because their hope is "the
hope promised by the Good News" (1:23), and since
that is based on the work of God in Christ, it is sure.

STUDY QUESTION: Paul presents the Colossians, and
us, an exalted image of Christ as
preexistent and divine. Does this
oppose or confirm the picture of
Jesus shown us in the Gospel of
Mark?

Colossians 1:24 – 2:5
THE GIFT AS MYSTERY

²⁴ It makes me happy to suffer for you, as I am suffering now, and in my own body to do what I can to make up all that has still to be undergone by Christ for the sake of his body, the Church.
²⁵ I became the servant of the Church when God made me responsible for delivering God's message to you, ·the message which was a mystery hidden for generations and centuries and has now
²⁷ been revealed to his saints. ·It was God's purpose to reveal it to them and to show all the rich glory of this mystery to pagans. The mystery is Christ
²⁸ among you, your hope of glory: ·this is the Christ we proclaim, this is the wisdom in which we thoroughly train everyone and instruct everyone,
²⁹ to make them all perfect in Christ. ·It is for this I struggle wearily on, helped only by his power driving me irresistibly.

¹ **2** Yes, I want you to know that I do have to struggle hard for you, and for those in Laodicea, and for so many others who have never
² seen me face to face. ·It is all to bind you together in love and to stir your minds, so that your under-

standing may come to full development, until you
3 really know God's secret ·in which all the jewels
of wisdom and knowledge are hidden.
4   I say this to make sure that no one deceives
5 you with specious arguments. ·I may be absent in
body, but in spirit I am there among you, de-
lighted to find you all in harmony and to see how
firm your faith in Christ is.

☩

The mention of Paul's mission in 1:23 provides the
opportunity for a further expression of concern for the
Colossians and a reemphasis of the message.

Even though the Colossian community had been
founded by Epaphras, and they had never seen Paul
"face to face" (2:1), he whose special call from God
was to be Apostle to the Gentiles (Ga 2:8) felt responsible for them. Although he was in prison, he and
Epaphras (cf. 4:12) kept on "struggling hard for
them" (2:1). Paul could not be there in person to
comfort them, but he could be present in spirit (2:5):
by his prayers (1:9), by his suffering for their sake
(1:24), and, most immediately, by this letter to them!

This reference to Paul's suffering is at first somewhat
strange. If the suffering of Christ has been efficacious
and complete (the point of 1:20), then how can Paul
in his sufferings "make up all that has still to be under-
gone by Christ"? (1:24). A rendering closer to the
Greek would be "the afflictions of Christ." Now, we
have already seen how Paul sees Christ and the Church
in the closest connection: the resurrected Lord is the

Head, It is the body (this represents a shift from
Paul's earlier language about the Church as Body of
Christ in 1 Co 12:12–27, Rm 12:4–5). Paul had to be
knocked off his horse to hear the word, "I am Jesus,
and you are persecuting me" (Ac 9:5), but he never
forgot that the Church remained the suffering presence
of Christ in the world whenever persecuted. So close
are Christ and those who believe in him that the
Church's sufferings can be called the "afflictions" of
Christ. In the New Testament, such afflictions seem inevitably to overtake those who belong to the Christ;
seem almost a sign that the Gospel is being effectively
preached in a hostile world. Paul constantly faced these
"afflictions" in his ministry (Rm 5:3, 8:35, 2 Co
1:4–8, 6:4, 7:4, Ph 1:17, 4:14) as did those who received the Gospel from him (1 Th 1:6, 2 Th 1:4, 2 Co
1:7, 8:2), just as Jesus had foretold (Mk 4:17, Mt
24:9).

Rejoicing in such afflictions is a paradox of faith, not
a form of masochism. Suffering is not good in itself.
Christians are able to rejoice when they suffer afflictions because their hope is secure. Even the deepest
and most subtle bodily and emotional agony cannot
threaten the worth of one whose value has been established by God. They can rejoice as well, knowing
that the Church is the body of Christ, the sacrament of
his continuing presence, and the suffering borne by the
Church is a share in his saving work for the world, a
sign of God's presence rather than his absence (cf.
1 P 1:7, 4:13, 5:9; Jm 1:2, Rm 5:1–5, 8:18–37, Mt
5:10–11).

The message of Paul to the Gentiles is a "Mystery"
(1:26), not only because God's way of reconciling the

world to himself was unknown to past ages (cf. Rm. 16:25, Ep 3:5), but also because it remains forever a gift of God's love beyond human comprehension or manipulation. Pious Jews, persecuted for their faith in the One God by Gentiles, had hoped for a "mystery" (as in Dn 2:28), in which God would restore sovereignty to Israel and condemn the godless Gentiles. This turned out to be too small a mystery for God. The Mystery of Christ proclaimed by Paul (cf. 1 Co 2:1) is that the Gentiles too have been called into the kingdom of God's love (Rm 11:25, Col 1:13). The mystery is "Christ among you (Gentiles)" (1:27). And having been so mysteriously reconciled to God through Christ, they have authentic hope: the hope of sharing completely in God's own life, which is his glory: "Christ among you, your hope of glory" (1:27, cf. 1:5, 1:23).

Paul has here returned to his central message to the Colossians. His instructions to them, as to everyone (1:28), is to seek maturity and perfection within this hope, not outside it. Incorporated into Christ, they are in touch with the power of God and the measure of authentic human perfection. Paul's concern for them begins to show more clearly: are they, in fact, being beguiled by smoother proposals?

There is a subtle monetary imagery running through this passage in the Greek. The mystery proclaimed by Paul is part of God's "economy" (1:25). God wills the Gentiles to know the "riches" of the mystery of Christ, to have all "richness" of knowledge and insight into the mystery (2:2). In Christ are hidden all the "treasures of wisdom and knowledge" (2:3). The Colossians, in a word, have a most precious possession in their faith, a treasure whose full worth is hidden now, but will be revealed later (3:4). It is their "hope stored up in heaven" (1:5).

Paul's characterization of the opponents is all the sharper when we recognize this imagery. They are first mentioned in 2:4. The *JB* translates, "Make sure that no one deceives you." Better would be, "Let no one defraud you." The opponents' clever words offer a better hope, but to follow them would be to lose the authentic treasure. Again, in 2:8, Paul speaks of the false teachers as "despoiling" or "plundering" the Colossians (*JB:* "trapping"). The Colossian Christians have been given the coin of God's realm; they should not chase after fool's gold.

STUDY QUESTIONS: Does Paul's insistence on the necessity and sufficiency of faith in Christ help or hinder relations with other believers in the One God, such as Jews and Moslems? For the sake of human unity, should Christians downplay the christocentrism of their faith?

Colossians 2:6 – 3:4
THE GIFT DEFENDED

⁶ You must live your whole life according to the
⁷ Christ you have received—Jesus the Lord; ·you
must be rooted in him and built on him and held
firm by the faith you have been taught, and full
of thanksgiving.

⁸ Make sure that no one traps you and deprives
you of your freedom by some secondhand,
empty, rational philosophy based on the principles of this world instead of on Christ.

⁹ In his body lives the fullness of divinity, and
¹⁰ in him you too find your own fulfillment, ·in the
one who is the head of every Sovereignty and
Power.

¹¹ In him you have been circumcised, with a
circumcision not performed by human hand, but
by the complete stripping of your body of flesh.

¹² This is circumcision according to Christ. ·You
have been buried with him, when you were baptized; and by baptism, too, you have been raised
up with him through your belief in the power of

¹³ God who raised him from the dead. ·You were
dead, because you were sinners and had not been

circumcised: he has brought you to life with him, he has forgiven us all our sins.

14   He has overridden the Law, and canceled every record of the debt that we had to pay; he has done
15 away with it by nailing it to the cross; ·and so he got rid of the Sovereignties and the Powers, and paraded them in public, behind him in his triumphal procession.

16   From now onward, never let anyone else decide what you should eat or drink, or whether you are to observe annual festivals, New Moons or sab-
17 baths. ·These were only pale reflections of what
18 was coming: the reality is Christ. ·Do not be taken in by people who like groveling to angels and worshiping them; people like that are always going on about some vision they have had, inflating themselves to a false importance with their worldly
19 outlook. ·A man of this sort is not united to the head, and it is the head that adds strength and holds the whole body together, with all its joints and sinews—and this is the only way in which it can reach its full growth in God.

20   If you have really died with Christ to the principles of this world, why do you still let rules dictate to you, as though you were still living in the
21 world? ·"It is forbidden to pick up this, it is forbidden to taste that, it is forbidden to touch some-
22 thing else"; ·all these prohibitions are only concerned with things that perish by their very use—an example of human doctrines and regulations!
23 It may be argued that true wisdom is to be found in these, with their self-imposed devotions, their self-abasement, and their severe treatment of the body; but once the flesh starts to protest, they are no use at all.

1 **3** Since you have been brought back to true life with Christ, you must look for the things that are in heaven, where Christ is, sitting at God's

2 right hand. ·Let your thoughts be on heavenly
   things, not on the things that are on the earth,
3 because you have died, and now the life you have
4 is hidden with Christ in God. ·But when Christ is
   revealed—and he is your life—you too will be revealed in all your glory with him.

✠

Although Paul rejoices in 2:5 at the stability of the
Colossians' faith, he immediately returns in 2:6 to the
necessity of standing firm in the Gospel message "just
as you have been taught." They are to be rooted in it,
built up on it, and hold firm to it. With this secure hope
in Christ, they can be full of thanksgiving (2:7; cf. also
1:12, 3:17). In order to strengthen their confidence in
the gift they have been given, Paul turns his attention
to the claims being made by those trying to lure the
Colossians away from their faith.

It is extraordinarily difficult to describe exactly the
position of the opponents. Paul's language is polemical;
we are not sure at times whether or not he is quoting
the opponents' slogans; he uses what seem to be technical religious terms of whose meaning we are no longer
sure; and throughout, there is a complex imagery pre-
sumed by both parties, the outlines of which we can
only partially surmise. But while the determination of
the opponents' precise teaching remains a fascinating
historical problem, the significant thing for us is Paul's
understanding of what they were saying and the implications he saw in their position; these issues we are

able to detect from the way Paul structures his argument.

From Paul's asides, we gather that these people (he never names them, and we are not sure they are members of the community) are making certain claims for themselves. The claims are based on a sort of religious philosophy which is traditional in nature (2:8); which demands dietary and sexual asceticism (2:16, 20–22); which calls for rigorous observance of the Law (probably the Law of Moses, together with their own ascetic prescriptions); and in which the worship of, or with, the Elemental Powers of the Universe (that is, the angels), plays a part (2:8,15,18). An odd mixture of elements, but in the syncretistic world of the first century, not unheard of. Indeed, there are so many plausible candidates that certain identification is not possible.

Some have noted that the language of 2:18 is similar to that used in pagan Mystery Cults, and suggest that the opponents were Christians attracted to the claims of salvation offered by them, with the assurance granted by "the vision they have had" in an initiation ceremony. Others suggest that Paul is responding to Jewish-Christians like those in Galatia (in whose observance of the Law of Moses, it will be recalled, submission to the Elements of the Universe and the keeping of special days were also involved, cf. Ga 3:19, 4:3,9). Still others have seen a resemblance to the ideas and practices of the Essenes. A recent and attractive proposal is that these opponents were a variety of rigorist Jewish mystics, whose sedulous observance of the Law and asceticism was complemented by a fer-

vent form of mysticism in which they "entered into
heaven" and "worshiped with the angels."

The important thing for Paul is that those who held
this position were making a claim to a greater maturity,
or perfection, not available to those whose faith was in
Christ alone. They claimed to be a kind of spiritual
elite, and from their lofty vantage could "judge" the
behavior of others (2:16) and even "disqualify" them
(2:18). They "deceive" and "entrap" others with these
claims (2:4,8).

Paul preemptorily rejects their claim to perfection.
He scorns their "philosophy" as "secondhand, empty"
(2:8), their claim of superiority on the basis of visions
as a "self-inflation" (2:18), and their rigorous asceticism as a showy self-abasement of no real use in
curbing the flesh (2:23). In fact, their whole outlook is
precisely "fleshly" in Paul's characteristic way of using
that term, to mean a sinful (and especially) hostile
outlook. Their arrogant, judgmental attitude shows that
their pretended maturity is just a subtle form of enslavement to their own desires. So also the Corinthians
who judged others showed themselves to be not spiritual but fleshly (1 Co 3:1–4). By keeping the Law so
scrupulously, they are not attaining a higher perfection.
They are running the risk of apostasy, for by seeking
this maturity by their own effort, they effectively deny
the value of Christ's saving act. Their philosophy is
"not according to Christ," but is an enslavement to the
angelic powers through whom the Law was given
(2:18; cf. Ga 3:19, 4:3). Their ritual observance is
an obeisance to what is illusory, for these are "only the
pale reflections of what was coming: the reality is
Christ" (2:17–18). The maturity they claim from vi-

sions is unreal, for by seeking a perfection outside
Christ, they "do not hold to the head" from which all
authentic growth in God comes (2:19).

Paul's positive argument (directed to the Colossians)
is twofold. First, he reminds them of what Christ accomplished by his death and resurrection (2:14–15).
The Law to which the opponents cling has not the
power to save, but only to condemn: it stood as a "record of the debt that we had to pay." By his saving
death, Christ destroyed the condemnatory power of the
Law—he "nailed it to the cross"—and rendered it null.
Paul's language here recalls such passages as Ga 2:19,
3:11–14, Rm 7:4–6, Ep 2:15–16. Furthermore, by
Christ's powerful resurrection into new life, he not only
demonstrated that the power of God was at work to
save, he also stripped those angelic powers (who were
seen as supporting the authority of the Law and who
demanded appeasement by its observance) of all their
dignity. They were but creatures in the first place
(1:16); their transcendent and threatening power was
granted only by those who served them. Christ by his
resurrection "paraded them in public, behind him in
his triumphal procession" (2:15). For similar language
about the triumph of Christ in his resurrection, cf. 1 P
3:21–22, Ph 2:9–10, Heb 1:3–4, Ep 1:19–20, 4:5–10.
Given this show of power, those who put their trust in
the Law and angels for their perfection are more to be
pitied than admired.

The second part of Paul's argument is to remind the
Colossians that they have been initiated into a Mystery
far superior to that of the pagans or the Jews, and have
gained a hope surer than that given by celestial visions.
The Mystery? Christ, "in whose body lives the fullness

of divinity" (2:9). Their initiation into the Mystery?
Baptism, superior to Jewish circumcision, since it removed not only a scrap of flesh, but the "whole body
of flesh," that is, the whole state of human alienation
from God.

Their initiation was an entering into the whole of
Christ's saving act. As he died on the cross, so did they
experience a death to their old self in baptism: "You
have been buried with him" (2:12). The consequence
of this is that, just as his death destroyed the inimical
force of the Law, so they who have entered into his
death need no longer "let rules dictate to them"
(2:20). They are free with the freedom given by God
(cf. Ga 5:1,13). But baptism has also initiated them
into the powerful risen life of Christ (2:12), and if this
is the case, they are to "look the things that are in
heaven, where Christ is" (3:1). Their life of faith and
their behavior is not to be governed by the demands of
the Law, which is earthly (2:20) and an enslavement;
but by the power which comes to them from the resurrected Christ (3:1), the power which alone is truly
life-giving, truly perfecting, in freedom. This initiation
into God's own life is not a spectacular affair: it is
"hidden in Christ." But when he appears, then the true
significance of their life of grace will be revealed: it is a
sharing in the glory of God (3:4).

Having shown the Colossians the true source of
fulfillment, and having reminded them of their incorporation into that fullness, Paul can now turn to giving
them still deeper insight into the mystery, by instruct-
ing them in what it means to "look for the things that
are in heaven" (3:1), what attitudes and actions
should characterize the Christian life.

STUDY QUESTIONS: How would Paul respond to a form
of piety which regarded perfection
as a matter of scrupulous observance of Church laws, rituals, and
feasts? Have Christians really
grasped the message of freedom
proclaimed by Paul?

Colossians 3:5–17
LIVING OUT THE GIFT

5 That is why you must kill everything in you that belongs only to earthly life: fornication, impurity, guilty passion, evil desires and especially greed, which is the same thing as worshiping a 6 false god; ·all this is the sort of behavior that 7 makes God angry. ·And it is the way in which you used to live when you were surrounded by 8 people doing the same thing, ·but now you, of all people, must give all these things up: getting angry, being bad-tempered, spitefulness, abusive lan- 9 guage and dirty talk; ·and never tell each other lies. You have stripped off your old behavior with 10 your old self, ·and you have put on a new self which will progress toward true knowledge the more it is renewed in the image of its creator; 11 and in that image there is no room for distinction between Greek and Jew, between the circumcised or the uncircumcised, or between barbarian and Scythian, slave and free man. There is only Christ: he is everything and he is in everything.
12 You are God's chosen race, his saints; he loves you, and you should be clothed in sincere compassion, in kindness and humility, gentleness and

13 patience. ·Bear with one another; forgive each
other as soon as a quarrel begins. The Lord has
14 forgiven you; now you must do the same. ·Over
all these clothes, to keep them together and com-
15 plete them, put on love. ·And may the peace of
Christ reign in your hearts, because it is for this
that you were called together as parts of one
body. Always be thankful.
16   Let the message of Christ, in all its richness,
find a home with you. Teach each other, and
advise each other, in all wisdom. With gratitude
in your hearts sing psalms and hymns and in-
17 spired songs to God; ·and never say or do anything except in the name of the Lord Jesus, giving thanks to God the Father through him.

✠

Christians have been set free from the Law by the
work of Christ. By being incorporated into his death
and resurrection by baptism, they have been given a
new nature. What is the way of life that is consonant
with this nature? It is important to note that Paul does
not replace the old law with a new code; there is no detailed list of directives, here. Rather, he wishes the
Colossians to grasp the fundamental attitudes which
should pervade their lives. He is confident that once
these basic attitudes are in place, appropriate action
will follow.

Paul picks up in 3:5 the life/death imagery he used
in speaking of baptism. Since the Colossians have been
given a new life as gift, it is fitting that they "kill" those
attitudes which dominated them when they were enslaved to sin and subject to God's wrath (for an under-

standing of this expression, cf. Rm 1:18–32). All the
vices Paul lists in 3:5 and 3:8 can bear the epitaph he
assigns to greed: "the same thing as worshiping a false
god." Their former alienation from God, caused by
their willful disobedience and distorted perception, led
them not only to pervert their natural human drives
(3:5), but to be alienated from each other in hostility,
spite, and abusiveness (3:8). Where our gods are the
projections of our desires, we cannot but be bitter competitors of each other.

Now Paul employs another traditional image associated with the baptismal ceremony: the taking off of
old clothes and the putting on of new symbolizes the
taking on of a new identity (cf. Rm 13:12, Ep
4:22–23, Jm 1:21, 1 P 2:1, Ga 3:27). The "stripping
off" of these selfish attitudes expresses the stripping off
of the "old self" (3:9). This is possible because they
have been clothed in baptism with a "new self," a new
identity, "which will progress toward true knowledge
the more it is renewed in the image of its creator"
(3:10). Christ, who is the "image of the unseen God"
(1:15), has restored true humanity to those who were
first created "in his image" (Gn 1:27).

What has been given us, as Paul says in another
place, is "the mind of Christ" (1 Co 2:16), which is
able to "transform us by the renewal of our minds"
(Rm 12:2). This is the path to authentic Christian maturity: allowing the Spirit of Christ, implanted within
us as the "word of truth" (Jm 1:18, 1 P 1:23, Col
1:5), to "grow and bear fruit" (Col 1:6,10, 4:12), in
an ever deeper and broader perception of the truth
about God's way with the world and with us.

And having been placed in a truthful relation with
God and the world, we need not lie to each other

(3:9). Rather, we can speak the truth, indeed, can speak such words of forgiveness as those spoken first to each of us by the Lord (3:13). Having the mind of Christ, we can recognize that divisions between races and classes of people are but human and not God's measurement, which is that Christ is all in all (3:11; cf. also Ga 3:27–28, 1 Co 12:13). And recognizing that by gift we have been reconciled to God and thereby to the world, we can for the first time regard other persons not as competitors for worth, but as fellow members of Christ's body. We are able for the first time to "put on" those qualities of gentleness and humility (3:12) which make us vulnerable to each other's demands and needs; able for the first time to "bear with one another" (3:13). In short, able for the first time to truly love, knowing that we have first been loved. And this, says Paul, is the completion, the perfection of Christian growth (3:14): not the Promethean ecstatic leap of the ascetic, but the reign of God's own peace achieved through the cross of Jesus (1:20) brought to life in the love within the body of the Church (3:15). It is this to which we have been called.

When the richness of this word of Christ has been truly perceived, there will inevitably be thanksgiving and praise offered to God the Father through the Lord Jesus, not only in prayers and hymns, but in every self-emptying gesture which spells that name (3:16–17). This section better repays meditation than analysis.

STUDY QUESTION: Every Easter, Christians renew their baptismal promises. Does baptism have for us the same pivotal importance in shaping our attitudes that it did for Paul?

Colossians 3:18 – 4:1
CHRISTIAN LIFE IN THE HOUSEHOLD

18 Wives, give way to your husbands, as you
19 should in the Lord. ·Husbands, love your wives
20 and treat them with gentleness. ·Children, be obedient to your parents always, because that is what
21 will please the Lord. ·Parents, never drive your
children to resentment or you will make them
feel frustrated.
22 Slaves, be obedient to the men who are called
your masters in this world; not only when you
are under their eye, as if you had only to please
men, but wholeheartedly, out of respect for the
23 Master. ·Whatever your work is, put your heart
into it as if it were for the Lord and not for men,
24 knowing that the Lord will repay you by making
you his heirs. It is Christ the Lord that you are
25 serving; ·anyone who does wrong will be repaid
in kind and he does not favor one person more
1 than another. 4 Masters, make sure that your
slaves are given what is just and fair, knowing
that you too have a Master in heaven.

✠

Christians may be those whose "homeland is in
heaven" (Ph 3:20) and who "look for the things that
are in heaven" (Col 3:1) while waiting for Christ their
life to appear, but they are also very much citizens of
this world as well, inevitable participants in the social
and political structures of their age.

How are those whose first allegiance is to a heavenly
Lord to regard the social structures within which they
find themselves? We don't find in the documents of the
New Testament a revolutionary ethic, or a program of
social change. Christianity is not first of all an ideol-
ogy. Even such potentially revolutionary visions as
"there is no room for distinction between Jew and
Greek, . . . slave and free man" (Col 3:11, and in Ga
3:28, "between male and female"), are not translated
by the New Testament writers into a social ethic. Indeed, the ethical teachings of the New Testament are
by and large conservative.

Why is this? It is partly due to the social status of
the first Christians. They were, after all, a relatively
powerless minority, whose impact on the larger social
structures could only be minimal. And as a threatened
and ostracized sect which already looked strange to
outsiders because of its beliefs, Christianity was eager
to reassure those in a position to crush them that their
behavior, at least, was no threat to earthly rulers or the
given order. Finally, most early Christians saw the social order then in place as a good one. It at least enabled them to exist.

But at a deeper level, the Gospel was aimed at the essential source of change, people's hearts. Social legislation, however enlightened, has given no one salvation. Indeed, as we have learned to our dismay, without the transformation of attitudes, even the best of social mechanisms have the power to destroy those they were meant to serve. The lack of attention given to social change in the New Testament does not legitimate the privatism of those Christians who ignore social and political inequities. Rather, it directs those who work for such change to the fundamental requirement: unless there is a new vision of humanity which is based on the truth about God and the world, no change in social structure will make a difference.

When Paul turned to the obligations of Christians within the basic societal unit of the Roman world, the Household, he found already at hand a long tradition of ethical teaching developed by Hellenistic moralists, both Greek and Jewish. The Household encompassed blood relatives, retainers and domestic servants, all under the complete authority of the *paterfamilias,* the Head of the Household. The teaching Paul used contained the mutual obligations of hierarchically arranged pairs: husband/wife, parent/child, master/slave, and the obligations of all to the *paterfamilias* of the household of the whole state, the Emperor. It was a rather static ethic, for the view of the world and society was static. It placed great emphasis on submission to authority, for it was considered that the recognition of one's place within the great scheme of things was an essential glue for holding together the civilized world.

Paul, and the other Christian writers who used this form of teaching (cf. also Ep 5:21 – 6:9, 1 P 2:13 –

3:7), were not thereby sacralizing a particular social order. Rather, within their given social structure (they could not have envisioned a Jeffersonian democracy), they employed the best ethical standards available. And they made distinctive modifications to this traditional teaching.

Here we see the strong emphasis Paul places on the mutuality of obligation, not simply in action, but in attitude. Corresponding to the wife's submissive spirit is the husband's obligation to have a loving and gentle attitude (3:18). Corresponding to the children's obedience is the father's obligation to encourage and not frustrate the children. More significantly, the motivation behind the obligations has been changed. Now, all is done "to please the Lord," "in the Lord," "fearing the Lord." This motivation changes everything. For if the submission of the woman is first of all to the Lord, then her submission to the man is thereby relativized. She cannot submit to him when this would displease the Lord, as when such submission would violate her conscience, the truth of the relationship, or the good of the community.

This relativization is seen most sharply in the case of the master/slave relationship. The slave is to be obedient, yes, but as one seeking to please the Lord, and as one receiving a reward from the Lord. The human master, in other words, is not the ultimate power recognized. In fact, these masters, too, have a "Master in heaven" to whom they must answer. The widest gap may separate the status of master and slave in society, but God "does not favor one person more than another" (3:25).

There is a tension between the deepest insights of

Paul into the implications of the mystery of Christ, and these ethical injunctions, between "there is neither slave nor free" (3:11) and "be submissive" (3:18). To ignore the tension would be to betray the truth. Yet, it is a tension which is itself creative, and bears within itself the potential of a deeper truth for the Church which continues to reflect on the meaning of Christian life within changing social settings.

STUDY QUESTION: How legitimate is it for a husband in our society to point to Col 3:18 as a justification for refusing to acknowledge his wife as an equal in every respect?

CHURCHES BECOMING THE CHURCH

2 Be persevering in your prayers and be thank-
3 ful as you stay awake to pray. ·Pray for us especially, asking God to show us opportunities for
announcing the message and proclaiming the
mystery of Christ, for the sake of which I am in
4 chains; ·pray that I may proclaim it as clearly as
I ought.
5 Be tactful with those who are not Christians
and be sure you make the best use of your time
6 with them. ·Talk to them agreeably and with a
flavor of wit, and try to fit your answers to the
needs of each one.
7 Tychicus will tell you all the news about me.
He is a brother I love very much, and a loyal
helper and companion in the service of the Lord.
8 I am sending him to you precisely for this purpose: to give you news about us and to reassure
9 you. ·With him I am sending Onesimus, that
dear and faithful brother who is a fellow citizen
of yours. They will tell you everything that is
happening here.
10 Aristarchus, who is here in prison with me,

sends his greetings, and so does Mark, the cousin of Barnabas—you were sent some instructions about him; if he comes to you, give him a warm
[11] welcome—·and Jesus Justus adds his greetings. Of all those who have come over from the Circumcision, these are the only ones actually working with me for the kingdom of God. They have been
[12] a great comfort to me. ·Epaphras, your fellow citizen, sends his greetings; this servant of Christ Jesus never stops battling for you, praying that you will never lapse but always hold perfectly
[13] and securely to the will of God. ·I can testify for him that he works hard for you, as well as for
[14] those at Laodicea and Hierapolis. ·Greetings from my dear friend Luke, the doctor, and also from Demas.
[15]   Please give my greetings to the brothers at Laodicea and to Nympha and the church which
[16] meets in her house. ·After this letter has been read among you, send it on to be read in the church of the Laodiceans; and get the letter from
[17] Laodicea for you to read yourselves. ·Give Archippus this message, "Remember the service that the Lord wants you to do, and try to carry it out."
[18]   Here is a greeting in my own handwriting— PAUL. Remember the chains I wear. Grace be with you.

✠

The final exhortations and greetings of this letter provide us with a fascinating glimpse of the sort of mutual communication and concern which bound together the first Christian communities. Just as the members of the Hellenistic household were bound together by mutual obligations (3:17 – 4:1), so were the disparate

Christian communities; and we are able to see, even within the lifetime of Paul, the beginning of the understanding that all the local congregations make up one, great Church. The concept of the Church as a worldwide, even a cosmic reality, making up the "one body of Christ" owed a great deal to the work and thought of Paul himself.

Paul's mission was not the solitary effort of an enthusiast, but the collective effort of many workers, directed by a skillful organizer. Paul did not work in isolation, but at the center of a far-flung network of fellow workers and delegates. By means of these delegates, he was able to maintain contact with communities throughout the Mediterranean world, to support them in their faith, and to rally their support for substantial practical projects, such as the relief-collection he organized for the Jerusalem community among the churches of Greece and Asia Minor (cf. Ga 2:10, 1 Co 16:1–3, 2 Co 8–9, Rm 15:22–32).

When we read Romans 16, we are surprised to find how many members of that community (which Paul had not yet visited) he knew by name. The same is true, here. Paul reports on the movements of, or sends greetings from, eight men whom he expects the Colossians to recognize by name, and he knows by name himself two important members of their community, Nympha and Archippus (4:15,17). It can be noted in passing, that both here and in Rm 16:1–3, women figure prominently among the leaders of the community. Many of the names found here occur also in the Letter to Philemon (2,23–24), which suggests a close relationship between the two letters.

That Paul saw himself in a position of authority over

the Colossian Church established by one of his delegates is indicated not only by the writing of this letter, but also by the directions he gives concerning Archippus (4:17) and Mark (4:10). He tells them that if Mark comes to them, they are to receive him. The hospitality shown by communities to the delegates, teachers, and pilgrims of other communities was not only a significant act of charity in a world where travel was frequent but accommodations either unavailable or disreputable (cf. Rm 12:13, Tt 1:8, 1 Tm 3:2, 1 P 4:9, Heb 13:2). It also signified the acceptance of the authority or teaching of the one who sent out such delegates (cf. Phm 21–22, 1 Co 16:10, 2 Jn 10, 3 Jn 5–10).

Fellowship was also maintained among communities by the exchange of letters written by leaders. Already in 1 Co 1:2, we see that Paul intended his letters to have a wider audience than that provided by a single church. Here, Paul tells the Colossians to share this letter with the Laodiceans, and themselves to read the letter he wrote to the Laodiceans (4:15–16). We no longer have the letter he wrote to the Laodiceans, though some have suggested that this may be the letter we call Ephesians. In any case, the exchange of letters between communities intensified their mutual awareness, and served to unify them in a common perception of their faith. Such exchange led to the writing of properly "encyclical" or circular letters, such as 1 Peter, James, and possibly, Ephesians.

Underlying this network of persons and letters was the conviction of sharing spiritually in the same hope, of being members of the same body of Christ, and of having the same mission to the world. As Paul hears of the faith and the difficulties of the Colossians from Epaphras, and responds with ceaseless prayer for them (1:3,9), so he expects them to pray for him as well. They are to remember his chains (4:18), and to pray that in spite of them, he and his fellow workers might find a way to proclaim the Gospel (4:2–3). And as Paul needs wisdom (1:28) to proclaim the Word effectively (4:4), so the Colossians require wisdom to know how to respond to those outside the fellowship who question them, and perhaps, challenge them (4:5–6; cf. also 1 P 3:15).

Paul signed this letter in his own handwriting (4:18). This may indicate that he had dictated the letter to a secretary, or even entrusted its formulation to a close fellow worker (cf. Rm 16:22, 1 Co 16:21, Ga 6:11, 2 Th 3:17); we cannot be sure. By signing it, however, Paul certified that it represented what he wanted to say to the Colossians, and having read this masterful letter ourselves, we can confidently agree that however distant Paul was "in the body," he brought himself very close "in spirit" (cf. 2:5).

STUDY QUESTION: Compare the ways the first Christians maintained communion with each other, and the sense of unity present in the parishes and dioceses of the contemporary Church.

The Letter to the Ephesian Church
The Church as the Place of Human Reconciliation

There is an obvious similarity in theme and expression between Ephesians and Colossians. But there are also significant differences, which arise from a shift in focus. Ephesians stands to Colossians much as Romans stands to Galatians. Paul, in Galatians, forged his teaching on justification by faith in the fire of controversy. Then, in Romans, he placed that teaching within a broader theological framework of God's will to save both Jews and Gentiles by grace. So also the polemic of Colossians concerning the superiority of the Mystery of Christ to any ersatz offer of salvation is placed, in Ephesians, within a magisterial reflection on the dimensions of this Mystery in a cosmic Church, which God has called into being by reconciling Jews and Gentiles to himself and therefore to each other.

The ancient and deep-rooted enmity between Jews and Gentiles, a hostility only exacerbated by the Law, was seen by Paul as a sign of the alienation between

God and humanity. When God reconciled humans to himself by the death and resurrection of Jesus, he called into being a new humanity, in which this divine/human reconciliation might be manifested in the reconciliation of humans in the Church. When Paul wrote Romans, he saw this reconciliation as not yet complete: the Jews, having rejected the Gospel of Christ, were in a state of enmity toward God. But, even then, he saw the dimensions of "this Mystery": that the rejection of the Jews would last only until "the whole pagan world has entered, and then after this the rest of Israel will be saved as well" (Rm 11:25–26). Now, in Ephesians, this mystery appears as something achieved: both Jews and Gentiles have access to God in the one Spirit (2:18). Has something happened between the writing of Romans and Ephesians to cause this shift in perspective? Or are Paul's statements colored by the fact that in Romans he did not want the Gentiles to boast over the Jews (Rm 11:13–32), whereas here, he wishes to stress their full incorporation into the promises, through the Gospel (Ep 3:6)? We do not know. But it is clear that there is a strong element of continuity between these two letters.

The Church stands at the center of Paul's reflection in Ephesians. The Church is the place where the mystery of God's will for humans is revealed, is, indeed, the bodying forth of that mystery in the world, insofar as within the community humans are truly reconciled to each other in the unity of the Spirit. That God has so created such a place of unity in the world is the cause of Paul's praise. It is also the point of his instruction. This unity is not only gift, it is also mandate. The Church must effectively realize and demonstrate this unity in the world, act as a sacrament of reconciliation, attracting all people into unity. Thus, the exhortations of Ephesians center on the community's need to realize this unity within itself, if it is to be the sign of God's unity in a divided world (cf. esp. 4:1–16).

The difficulties of understanding Ephesians stem less from the complexity of its argument than the richness of its language and imagery. The language is elaborate and sometimes redundant, with a piling up of synonyms and lengthy clauses. This style is not totally unlike that of Paul's other letters, but is nowhere found in such a concentrated form. The images accumulate rapidly, and almost defy analysis. At times, as in Colossians, the images seem to presuppose a background we can only partially reconstruct. Many of them are rooted in common Christian traditions associated with baptism, but others appear to show the influence of the various meditations on wisdom found in the Old Testament as well as contemporary Jewish writings.

The liturgical sound of the language in Ephesians is not accidental, for the whole tone of the letter is prayerful. Indeed, the passages in Paul's other writings which come closest to the Ephesian style are those of prayer and thanksgiving (e.g. Rm 1:2–7, 16:25–27, 1 Co 1:4–9, 2 Co 1:3–7). Ephesians stands as a reminder that the function of theology is not simply to analyze or criticize; it is, finally, to move to praise.

Of all the Pauline letters, Ephesians offers the fewest clues to the circumstances of its composition. Although in the form of a letter, it contains little concrete information either about Paul or the recipients. Paul is a prisoner (3:1,13, 6:20), and is about to send Tychicus as a deliverer of news and comfort (6:21). These remarks strikingly resemble the personal notices of Col 4:2,7, and are, by comparison, somewhat colorless and formal. None of the recipients is mentioned individually, and the few warnings against false teaching (4:14, 5:6–11) are vague and general. In fact, the teachings and exhortations throughout are general in tone, as though the document was addressed to a wider audience of Gentiles (the "you" of the letter, in contrast to the "we" of the Jewish believers), than those of a particular community. This does not seem to be a letter written in response to an immediate crisis.

This formal tone is the more surprising if the letter is really written to the Ephesians, for that community was one Paul stayed in for a considerable period, and knew well (cf. Ac 19:10, 20:17–35, 1 Co 15:32, 16:8). It would not be like Paul to leave unmentioned the experiences shared with a community firsthand. Actually, it is not at all certain that the Ephesians were the intended recipients of the letter. Although many of the Greek manuscripts have the words "in Ephesus" following "to the saints" in the greeting, many of the most ancient and trustworthy manuscripts lack any place name, even though the construction of the Greek sentence and normal epistolary usage would seem to demand one. The *JB* follows these manuscripts in eliminating the place name from its translation of the greeting (1:1). But if not to the Ephesians, to whom? Scholars (ancient and modern) have suggested either that another name originally stood in this place (the second-century writer, Marcion, guessed it was the missing letter to the Laodiceans; cf. Col 4:16), or that, from the beginning, this was intended to be a circular letter, read in many churches.

Our lack of certainty regarding the circumstances of the letter should have the salutary effect of turning our attention to the text of the document itself. Ephesians demonstrates as well as any writing of the New Testament that the occasion or even the purpose for writing scarcely exhausts the meaning of the text. Whether Paul wrote this letter himself or through an associate, whether it was addressed to one community or to many; whether, indeed, it was written by followers of Paul after his death, matters little. Ephesians stands among the maturest flowerings of the Apostle's witness to Christ alive in the Church, and testifies as directly to us as to those unknown Gentiles for whom it was first written.

Ephesians 1:1–14
GOD HAS BLESSED US IN CHRIST

¹ 1 From Paul, appointed by God to be an apostle of Christ Jesus, to the saints who are faith-
² ful to Christ Jesus: ·Grace and peace to you
from God our Father and from the Lord Jesus
Christ.

³ Blessed be God the Father of our Lord Jesus
Christ,
   who has blessed us with all the spiritual blessings of heaven in Christ.
⁴ Before the world was made, he chose us, chose
us in Christ,
   to be holy and spotless, and to live through love
   in his presence,
⁵ determining that we should become his adopted
   sons, through Jesus Christ
   for his own kind purposes,
⁶ to make us praise the glory of his grace,
   his free gift to us in the Beloved,
⁷ in whom, through his blood, we gain our freedom, the forgiveness of our sins.
   Such is the richness of the grace
⁸ which he has showered on us

in all wisdom and insight.

9 He has let us know the mystery of his purpose,
the hidden plan he so kindly made in Christ
from the beginning

10 to act upon when the times had run their
course to the end:
that he would bring everything together under
Christ, as head,
everything in the heavens and everything on
earth.

11 And it is in him that we were claimed as God's
own,
chosen from the beginning,
under the predetermined plan of the one who
guides all things
as he decides by his own will;

12 chosen to be,
for his greater glory,
the people who would put their hopes in Christ
before he came.

13 Now you too, in him,
have heard the message of the truth and the
good news of your salvation,
and have believed it;
and you too have been stamped with the seal of
the Holy Spirit of the Promise,

14 the pledge of our inheritance
which brings freedom for those whom God has
taken for his own,
to make his glory praised.

✠

The special tone of Ephesians is evident at once. In
this solemn prayer of blessing, Paul reveals to his
readers his insight into the mystery of the faith (cf.

3:3–4), and shows them the proper goal of the knowledge of God, the praise of Him (1:6,12,14).

The prayer of blessing (in Hebrew, *Berakah*) is the
prayer *par excellence* both of Judaism and Christianity.
Throughout the Old Testament (e.g. 1 K 1:48, 5:7,
8:15, 2 Ch 2:12, Dn 2:20–23, Ps 18:46, 28:6, 106:
48, etc.) and the New Testament (e.g. Lk 1:68, Rm
1:25, 9:5, 2 Co 1:3–7), we find God's people responding to his action among them with the blessing of his
name. Frequently short and spontaneous formulae of
blessing are used (e.g. Gn 24:27, Ex 18:10, 1 S
25:32). Other times the blessings have greater solem-
nity and length (e.g. Tb 8:15–17, 13:1–18, 1 Ch 29:
10–13, 1 P 1:3–5). Such benedictions shaped the
prayer of the synagogue (the "eighteen benedictions")
and the Church (the Eucharistic prayers). They also
express the essential human vocation before God. All of
human existence should be a blessing of his name.

There are usually three parts to this kind of prayer:
an opening statement of praise ("Blessed be God"),
followed by the reasons for the praise ("who has
blessed us"), concluded by a final statement of praise
("alleluia, Blessed be God," "amen," or the like). The
third element is somewhat disguised in this Ephesian
blessing, but can be spotted in the threefold "to the
praise of his glory" in 1:6,12,14. The structure of the
prayer is not arbitrary. How can God be blessed by humans, except by the remembrance of how he has
blessed us? And the gratitude we feel for such blessing
moves spontaneously to renewed thanksgiving for the
gift.

The wealth of meaning in this prayer yields only to
repeated reading and reflection, but it is possible to

point out some of its features. As we read through the
prayer, we see that verses 4 through 14 make explicit
what is stated in verse 3: "He has blessed us with all
the spiritual blessings of heaven in Christ." There are
two points to notice, here. The blessings are "spiritual": they have little to do with material gain and pros-
perity, and everything to do with our life before God in
the world. And all these blessings are given to us "in
Christ" and "through Christ." As in Colossians, the
centrality of Christ's role is emphasized. Not only have
we been freed from sin by Christ's saving death on the
cross (1:7); he has also been the agent of our being
chosen as part of God's people (1:11); and through
him we have become God's adopted sons (1:5).

But even more than in Colossians, Paul here refers
all to the work of God the Father. Every blessing
which has come to us "in Christ" comes from the Father as free gift (1:6) which he has lavishly showered
on us (1:7). More than that, everything which has
happened to us has come about as a result of God's
plan for the world. Here, we enter the distinctiveness of
Ephesians' teaching on the Mystery.

Already in Rm 8:28-30, Paul had written, "We
know that by turning everything to their good God co-
operates with all those who love him, with all those
that he has called according to his purpose. They are
the ones he chose specially long ago and intended to
become true images of his Son, so that his Son might
become the eldest of many brothers. He called those he
intended for this; those he called he justified, and with
those he justified he shared his glory." Here, in Ephesians, we find the same emphasis on "God's purpose."
We read, repeatedly: "for his own kind purposes"

(1:5); "the mystery of his purpose, the hidden plan he so kindly made in Christ" (1:9); "under the predetermined plan of the one who guides all things as he decides by his own will (1:11).

We should note at once that this talk of "God's will" has nothing to do with the fate of individuals, as in some teachings on predestination. Rather, Paul is telling us that by grasping what has been given us in Christ, we are able to glimpse that side of the face of God which is turned always toward the world in love, and in the light of this gift, we are able to discern what he always intended for the world.

That God had chosen from the beginning a people for himself, and that he had done so in view of the Messiah, would not have sounded strange to the Jews of Paul's time, "the people who would put their hopes in Christ before he came" (1:12). This awareness of election by God to be his special people was the glory of the Jews, and their boast (cf. Rm 2:17–20, 3:1–2, 9:1–5). Nor would the assignment of "headship" to the Messiah at the end of the ages be astonishing to them, for God's anointed one was to rule over the age to come (cf. e.g. Dn 7:13–14). What was new and unheard of in Paul's proclamation of the mystery is that God's call and election in Christ extended to all people, including the despised Gentiles (cf. 3:6).

In verse 13, the Gentiles are the "you" whom Paul addresses. No less than the Jews who believed in Christ, they have been called to be God's people. They have believed in "the Gospel of salvation", they have been sealed with the Messianic Spirit (the "Holy Spirit of the Promise"), they have been given that freedom which is the gift given to those who are children and heirs (1:14; cf. Ga 3:7, Rm 8:14–15), and are able, as members of God's special people, to "make his glory praised" (cf. Is 43:20, 1 P 2:9).

This is "news" indeed, and Good News for the Jews as well as for the Gentiles. The calling of Gentiles into his people signals that God's reconciling work in the world is truly effective. Paul will develop this later in the letter (2:11–22).

If we are to hear this news as freshly as did those Gentiles whom Paul addressed, we must wrench ourselves out of the bored habituation of piety and allow ourselves to see the world as they did. In a world of totalitarian rule and crumbling communities, the meaning of life and of history was hard to come by. In the religious literature of that age, we see how human life appeared as insignificant, subject to the whims of chance and the crushing force of fate. Philosophers could speak of a benign providence, true, but this philosophic serenity offered little comfort against the knock of Caesar's agents at the door. Religious cults offered a freedom from fate, but it was a freedom only of individuals, and fate's hand was not thereby weakened.

For these pagans, the message that the passage of time was not the despair of meaningless repetition, but the progress of the world toward a goal; that there was, in fact, a meaning to human existence, and a meaning available to them by gift; that all which happened came about as a result of the loving plan of a God who was a Father seeking among humanity a people truly free with the freedom of God's children; this message was news of surpassing goodness.

But perhaps we need not imagine ourselves as ancient pagans to hear this message. We live in a world no less fragmented, no less threatening than that of the Roman Empire. We hear many and competing explanations for the movement of events, from the cosmic progress of dialectical materialism to the ludicrous claims of biorhythms and astrology. And all around us, we find people frantically seeking to escape the confinement of their lives, by inner enlightenment or communal fellowship. The message that the history of the world finds its meaning and goal in Christ is just as paradoxical and scandalous today as ever. It may be a message of comfort to those who believe, but in the face of hard experience, not an easy comfort.

STUDY QUESTION: How does Paul's way of talking about "God's will" in this passage compare to the way we use that expression in reference to the events of our lives?

Ephesians 1:15 – 2:10
THE KNOWLEDGE OF THE POWER OF GOD

15   That will explain why I, having once heard
about your faith in the Lord Jesus, and the love
16 that you show toward all the saints, ·have never
failed to remember you in my prayers and to
17 thank God for you. ·May the God of our Lord
Jesus Christ, the Father of glory, give you a spirit
of wisdom and perception of what is revealed, to
18 bring you to full knowledge of him. ·May he enlighten the eyes of your mind so that you can see
what hope his call holds for you, what rich glo-
19 ries he has promised the saints will inherit ·and
how infinitely great is the power that he has exercised for us believers. This you can tell from the
20 strength of his power ·at work in Christ, when he
used it to raise him from the dead and to make
21 him sit at his right hand, in heaven, ·far above
every Sovereignty, Authority, Power, or Domination, or any other name that can be named,
not only in this age but also in the age to come.
22 He has put all things under his feet, and made
him, as the ruler of everything, the head of the
23 Church; ·which is his body, the fullness of him
who fills the whole creation.

¹ ² 2 And you were dead, through the crimes and
the sins ·in which you used to live when you
were following the way of this world, obeying
the ruler who governs the air, the spirit who is at
³ work in the rebellious. ·We all were among them
too in the past, living sensual lives, ruled entirely
by our own physical desires and our own ideas;
so that by nature we were as much under God's
⁴ anger as the rest of the world. ·But God loved us
with so much love that he was generous with his
⁵ mercy: ·when we were dead through our sins, he
brought us to life with Christ—it is through grace
⁶ that you have been saved—·and raised us up with
him and gave us a place with him in heaven, in
Christ Jesus.
⁷   This was to show for all ages to come, through
his goodness toward us in Christ Jesus, how infi-
⁸ nitely rich he is in grace. ·Because it is by grace
that you have been saved, through faith; not by
anything of your own, but by a gift from God;
⁹ not by anything that you have done, so that no-
¹⁰ body can claim the credit. ·We are God's work of
art, created in Christ Jesus to live the good life as
from the beginning he had meant us to live it.

✠

Paul's prayer of blessing becomes one of thanksgiving to God for the way the Ephesians have accepted the
"message of the truth" (1:13), and, as frequently in
his letters, this thanksgiving provides a transition to the
teaching. The prayer resembles Col 1:3–12: Paul has
not seen this community firsthand, but has only heard
of their faith in the Lord Jesus and their love toward
all the saints (i.e. other Christians), and, having heard,

gives thanks. In the prayer, Paul shows the way he would like to see that faith and love grow; we are not surprised to find him saying that the growth must emerge from the gift already given.

God has already graced them with "all wisdom and insight" (1:8); now, Paul prays that God will give them a "spirit of wisdom and perception" so that they can come to full knowledge of him (1:17). Such knowledge of God is clearly not abstract or theoretical; it is experiential. It is available to them only because God has shown himself in the person and work of Jesus, and the gift of the Holy Spirit. Having experienced these, their eyes have been enlightened (1:18).

We meet here for the first time in Ephesians the light/darkness, life/death imagery we saw in Colossians, and which formed an important part of the traditional teaching on baptism. Later in the letter, Paul will tell them that they were once "children of darkness" but now are "children of the light," and that therefore they should act as those in the light (5:8–14). It is, in fact, Paul's mission to "enlighten all men" concerning the Mystery of Christ (3:9). The enlightenment comes not from him, but from Christ: "Christ will shine on you" (5:14).

The ancient world, no less than our own, had many religious and philosophical movements which promised "enlightenment." Frequently, this meant that people came to a realization of some spark of divinity which was theirs by nature, but which had been hidden by the tragic mistake of the body. With the "knowledge" of their true being, they could escape the confines of their bodily existence, and realize their share in the divine. Not so far removed, really, from the secular enlightenment movements of our own day, like EST, which hold out to the troubled the easy salvation of "self-realization." But the enlightenment of which Paul speaks is not a form of "self-realization." It is that new perception of reality which comes from acknowledging it as a gift. The Ephesians are to come to fuller knowledge of "what is revealed" (1:17).

Paul wants them to grasp three things, which are really one. First, the "hope his call holds for you" (1:18). The triad of faith/hope/love is once more complete (cf. Col 1:5), and we recognize again that when Paul speaks of hope, he has in mind not just a subjective feeling, but the objective reality which makes that attitude appropriate. The faith and love of the Ephesians are based in something real: the hope, which is the anticipation of the full gift of salvation, has been given them already by way of pledge in the bestowal of the Holy Spirit (1:13). This gift of the Spirit is like a down payment; it stands as surety for the full inheritance of God's life, called "glory" (1:14). The second thing that Paul wants the Ephesians to realize, consequently, is "the rich glories he has promised the saints will inherit" (1:18). Why is the hope real and the inheritance certain? The third thing for them to realize is "the infinitely great power that he has exercised for us believers" (1:19). The gift given to believers is not just teachings or ideals; it is a gift of *power*. What power? The power which is God's own life. There are many forms of power in the world, and many claimants to human allegiance. But there is but one ultimate and all-encompassing power which creates, sustains, and enlivens. And when this is at work, there is transformation.

The sign that God's power is truly at work among them is the awesome display of might revealed in the resurrection of Jesus from the dead (1:20–23). We would miss Paul's thought here, if we failed to see that he is drawing the tightest possible connection between what happened in Jesus and what happens in those who believe, between the power at work in the resurrection and the power at work in the Church. His description of the power revealed in the resurrection provides the basis for all he says in 2:1–10.

That a man should be raised from the dead is indeed a sign of God's power, for who can give life but God? Jesus' resurrection, though, was more than a resuscitation; it was an entering into a new form of existence, in which he shared fully in the life and power of God. This exaltation was seen by the first Christians as an enthronement. The phrase, "make him sit at his right hand" (1:20), is from Psalm 110:1, which was used from the first by the Christians to express the reality of the resurrection: "The Lord said to my Lord, 'Sit at my right hand and I make your enemies a footstool for you'" (cf. Ac 2:34–35, 1 Co 15:25, Heb 1:13, 1 P 3:22). In a real sense, Jesus became "Lord" by the resurrection (Ac 2:36, Ph 2:9–11, Rm 1:4), that is, he came into his full share of the Father's own power and dominion over all creation. And because this is the ultimate power, all other forces in the universe are thereby dramatically revealed as powerless (cf. Col 2:10,15; 1 P 3:22, Ph 2:9–10). Even those angelic powers whom people hold in awe are "put under his feet." This last phrase recalls Ps 8:4–6: "Ah, what is man that you should spare a thought for him, the son of man that you should care for him? Yet you have made him little less than a god, you have crowned him with glory and splendor, made him lord over the work of your hands, set all things under his feet." The Psalmist was thinking only of the fragility and dignity of humankind. The first Christians saw in Jesus the perfect fulfillment of these verses, for he was the "son of man" who suffered for others, and was then established as Lord by the resurrection (cf. Heb 2:5-9).

Verses 22-23 are difficult to understand, since the Greek is at once pregnant and ambiguous. As the son of man of Psalm 8 was made lord over the works of God's hand, Jesus is here said to be made "ruler of everything, the head of the Church." It is possible to render the Greek in a number of ways, including "head over all things, for the sake of the Church," or "in the Church." The ambiguity does not lie in the dominion of Christ; that is clear enough. Nor is there any doubt that Christ is "head," that is, source of authority and life, over believers (cf. 1 Co 11:3, Col 1:18). But what is the relationship between the two? It would seem, from what Paul says later, that the rule Christ exercises in the Church is at once a manifestation of his cosmic domination, and a sign to those forces yet unwilling to acknowledge it (2:7, 3:10). The Church is the place where Christ's rule is made actual. It is in this sense that Paul can speak of the Church as "the fullness of him who fills the whole creation" (1:23). The Church adds nothing to the stature of Christ, but provides the sign that his rule is active. The Church's nature and mission is to "body forth" in the world that life which comes from the head. This is obviously an exalted role Paul assigns to the Church. It is not a cause for self-congratulation, for it is only to the extent that the Church manifests that dominion and life in its midst that it in fact becomes the Church.

The pertinence of Paul's emphasis on the power of Christ's resurrection at work in the Church becomes clear in 2:1–10. Just as Christ had died, so were the believers formerly like dead people in their sins (2:1,5). And just as Christ was raised, so have they, in baptism, been brought to life by the power of God, raised with him and given a place with him in heaven (2:5–6). In speaking of their former sinful way of life as a "death" Paul points to more than their individual sinfulness. As in Romans 1–2 and Colossians 1, he is talking about humanity's alienation from God. Refusing to acknowledge the true God, they were in a state of rebellion, and were subjected to inimical spiritual forces (2:2). This subjection to evil manifested itself in their whole way of life: in the way they used their drives and desires and perceptions in patterns of compulsive self-aggrandizement. Lives like these could not but be self-destructive, a kind of living death.

What is remarkable about Paul's presentation here is the way he includes Jews as well as Gentiles in this state of alienation from God. Notice the constant shift between "you" (the Gentiles) and "we" (the Jews) in this passage. As in Romans 2–3, Paul asserts firmly that all have turned away from the true God, and all stand equally in need of the salvation which comes from him.

In the opening blessing, Paul praised the "richness of the grace which he has showered on us . . . his free gift to us in the Beloved" (1:8,6). Here, he repeatedly stresses that the salvation which has come to Jew and Gentile alike is completely gratuitous, totally gift. It is "not by anything that you have done" (2:9), for if it were, we could "claim the credit." No, authentic life can come only from God: "It is through grace that you have been saved" (2:5,8). And, Paul adds, "through faith" (2:8). But faith is not an achievement separate from the gift; it is precisely the willingness to accept life as his gift, to recognize that both by creation and redemption in Christ "we are God's work of art," and that the good deeds we perform are not a replacement of his grace but an expression of it (2:10). The best commentary a reader could find for these extraordinarily rich ten verses would be the first eight chapters of Paul's Letter to the Romans.

STUDY QUESTION: It has proven difficult for Christians through the ages to accept Paul's teaching that we are saved completely by gift and not by our own efforts. What is there within us which resists this message?

Ephesians 2:11–22
THE UNITY OF JEW AND GENTILE IN THE CHURCH

11 Do not forget, then, that there was a time when you who were pagans physically, termed the Uncircumcised by those who speak of themselves as the Circumcision by reason of a physical 12 operation, ·do not forget, I say, that you had no Christ and were excluded from membership of Israel, aliens with no part in the covenants with their Promise; you were immersed in this 13 world, without hope and without God. ·But now in Christ Jesus, you that used to be so far apart from us have been brought very close, by the 14 blood of Christ. ·For he is the peace between us, and has made the two into one and broken down the barrier which used to keep them apart, actually destroying in his own person the hostility 15 caused by the rules and decrees of the Law. This was to create one single New Man in himself out of the two of them and by restoring peace 16 through the cross, to unite them both in a single Body and reconcile them with God. In his own 17 person he killed the hostility. ·Later he came to bring the good news of peace, peace to you who

were far away and peace to those who were near
18 at hand. ·Through him, both of us have in the one
Spirit our way to come to the Father.
19   So you are no longer aliens or foreign visitors:
you are citizens like all the saints, and part of
20 God's household. ·You are part of a building that
has the apostles and prophets for its foundations,
and Christ Jesus himself for its main cornerstone.
21 As every structure is aligned on him, all grow
22 into one holy temple in the Lord; ·and you too,
in him, are being built into a house where God
lives, in the Spirit.

✠

In a breathtaking equation, Paul insists that the alienation of people from God means alienation of people from each other. The classic expression of this alienation is the division between Jews and non-Jews
(Gentiles). In his day, these were regarded as the "two
races" of the civilized world, and they were separated
by more than ethnic differences. For some time, there
had been sporadic but intense cultural and religious ri-
valry between them, and relations were not good.

Although Jews lived everywhere in the Roman Empire, neither they nor their neighbors saw them as having any real allegiance to the cities in which they lived.
The Jews belonged first of all to "Israel," a religious
fellowship, to be sure, but with real economic, religious
and political ties to the Holy Land, where the Temple
stood as the sign of the unity of all Jews throughout the
world. They were a people chosen specially by God for
covenanting, and enjoyed special privileges before God

as a result: they received his words through Law and
Prophets, they were to be heirs of the promises, they
were the ones who "hoped in the Christ before he
came" (1:12; cf. Rm 2:17-18, 3:1-2, 9:1-5). They
were "near" to God (2:17). But they were also distant
from their Gentile neighbors, a distance signaled by the
physical rite of circumcision, and the observance of the
Law of Moses.

The resentment the Gentiles felt toward this
"different people" was only fueled by the Jewish claims
to religious and cultural superiority (Rm 2:17-18).
Though God had chosen this people to be the first
fruits of a larger harvest (Jr 2:3), to be a "light to the
Gentiles" which would attract all peoples to the worship of the true God (Is 42:6, 49:6), and had given
the Law as a sign to all the nations of his will (Dt
4:6), so that all might turn to him and the whole earth
be filled with the knowledge of the Lord (Is 11:9), this
is not the way it turned out. Some Jews held to their
gifts from God as possessions meant only for them.
The Gentiles were excluded from the "membership of
Israel, aliens with no part in the covenants with their
Promises . . . without hope and without God" (2:12).
In their own eyes, and in the eyes of the Jews, the Gentiles were "far apart" from Israel, and therefore from
God (2:13,17). Paul calls the relations between Jew
and Gentile a state of "hostility" (2:14,16). Alienation
from God is seen most clearly in the division between
people on the basis of religion.

The hostility was expressed concretely in the arrangement of the Temple in Jerusalem, the place of
God's presence, where the people gained "access" to
him through prayer and sacrifice. The Temple had a

court for Gentiles, but they were excluded from the
inner court, which was reserved for those who were circumcised and kept the Law. The Gentiles did not have
full cultic "access" to God. Between the courts was this
sign: "No man of another nation is to enter . . . and
whoever is caught will have himself to blame that his
death ensues." What a graphic image! Here, in the
place where God could be approached, a whole part of
humanity was excluded on pain of death. The Law
which had been intended as an invitation to all nations
had become a "barrier" between peoples, a wall of division as real and baleful as the sign on the Temple
wall.

This division, Paul says, was not at all what God intended. The work of Christ, climaxed and fulfilled by
his death, was to heal the alienation between God and
humanity, to "make peace" by his blood (cf. Col
1:20). In a word, by Christ's death, God made a new
covenant with all people (cf. Ex 24:3–8, Heb
9:11–15). Where there is covenant, there is peace between the covenanting parties. But Christ is not simply
the "peace" between us and God, he is also the "peace
between us" humans (2:14). By dying under the curse
of the Law (Ga 3:10–14), and by being raised by the
power of the Father as Lord (1:19–23), Jesus nullified
the religious power of the Law, and destroyed its ability to stand as a barrier between people before God
(2:14–15). The man Jesus revealed to us a whole new
way of being human. By his obediential faith in his Father, he showed us that humans are not defined by the
laws they keep, but by the trust they show toward God.
The faith he demonstrated has, in virtue of his resurrection, been made available to us by the outpouring of

the Holy Spirit. And in this is true "access" to God. It is an "access" open equally to Jews and Gentiles, for it has not come about through human effort but by the free gift of the Spirit: "Through him, both of us have in the one Spirit our way to come to the Father" (2:17).

God has constituted in Jesus a "New Man" in whom Jews and Gentiles are at peace. In this act of God, Paul sees the fulfillment of the promise spoken long ago through the prophet Isaiah, "peace, peace to far and near, says the Lord" (Is 57:19), and he applies this proclamation of peace to the two parties. Through Jesus' death, "those who were near" (the Jews) were established in the covenantal peace promised them; and through the proclamation of the Gospel, "those who were far off" (the Gentiles) have been given that same peace (2:13,17). And more: they who were before strangers to the people of God (2:13,19) have been made "citizens like all the saints, and part of God's household" (2:19). What Paul means by this household of God is, of course, precisely the Christian community. It is here that the enmity between Jew and Greek has been for the first time resolved, through the acceptance by both of the Good News from God in Jesus Christ. The something that does not like a wall turns out to be someone, who is God.

Corresponding to the Temple of Jerusalem, which symbolized the alienation between Jew and Gentile, Paul describes the community of faith as a new form of temple, a living temple which symbolizes the unity created by the Spirit. We see traces of this temple imagery for the Church elsewhere in Paul (cf. 1 Co 3:16–17, 6:19–21, 2 Co 6:14–7:1), and in other

New Testament writings (Heb 10:21, 1 P 2:5). It is like the image of the body, in that the life and growth of the community is seen as completely dependent on Christ: he is its "main cornerstone," the fundamental point of departure for any construction (2:20–21). Those who have preached Christ, the "apostles and prophets" have proclaimed "the stone rejected by the builders, that proved to be the keystone" (Ps 118:22; cf. Mt 21:42, Ac 4:11, 1 P 2:7). This is the proclamation of the dead and risen Messiah, which is the basis of the Christian faith. Paul says in another place, "no other foundation can anyone lay than that which is laid, which is Christ Jesus" (1 Co 3:11). Insofar as the Christian preachers "like skilled master builders" (1 Co 3:10) laid this foundation, they can themselves be regarded as part of the "foundations" for the spiritual temple which is the Church, not by their personality, but by their proclamation.

STUDY QUESTIONS: The Church today is made up almost entirely of those formerly called Gentiles. Has the Church erected its own wall against the Jews? What building blocks do we contribute by our own attitudes?

Ephesians 3:1–21
THE MYSTERY OF GOD'S LOVE

¹ ² 3 So I, Paul, a prisoner of Christ Jesus for the sake of you pagans . . . ·You have probably heard how I have been entrusted by God with the
³ grace he meant for you, ·and that it was by a revelation that I was given the knowledge of the mys-
⁴ tery, as I have just described it very shortly. ·If you read my words, you will have some idea of the depths that I see in the mystery of Christ.
⁵ This mystery that has now been revealed through the Spirit to his holy apostles and prophets was
⁶ unknown to any men in past generations; ·it means that pagans now share the same inheritance, that they are parts of the same body, and that the same promise has been made to them, in
⁷ Christ Jesus, through the gospel. ·I have been made the servant of that gospel by a gift of grace from God who gave it to me by his own power.
⁸ I, who am less than the least of all the saints, have been entrusted with this special grace, not only of proclaiming to the pagans the infinite
⁹ treasure of Christ ·but also of explaining how the mystery is to be dispensed. Through all the ages,

this has been kept hidden in God, the creator of
10 everything. Why? ·So that the Sovereignties and
Powers should learn only now, through the
Church, how comprehensive God's wisdom really
11 is, ·exactly according to the plan which he had
had from all eternity in Christ Jesus our Lord.
12 This is why we are bold enough to approach God
in complete confidence, through our faith in him;
13 so, I beg you, never lose confidence just because
of the trials that I go through on your account:
they are your glory.
14   This, then, is what I pray, kneeling before the
15 Father, ·from whom every family, whether spiritual or natural, takes its name:
16   Out of his infinite glory, may he give you the
power through his Spirit for your hidden self
17 to grow strong, ·so that Christ may live in your
hearts through faith, and then, planted in love
18 and built on love, ·you will with all the saints
have strength to grasp the breadth and the length,
19 the height and the depth; ·until, knowing the love
of Christ, which is beyond all knowledge, you are
filled with the utter fullness of God.
20   Glory be to him whose power, working in us,
can do infinitely more than we can ask or imag-
21 ine; ·glory be to him from generation to generation in the Church and in Christ Jesus for ever
and ever. Amen.

☩

There are four paradoxes in this chapter. That God
should give life to humanity through the death of a
man is so much a paradox it quite goes beyond anything the world can recognize as wisdom; it appears as
foolishness (1 Co 1:18–25). But precisely this foolish-

ness is the secret God has kept hidden for all ages (1 Co 2:7), to be revealed in the preaching of the cross. That God should choose the proclamation of this crucified Messiah as the means to reconcile Jew and Gentile again appears as paradox, for precisely this proclamation has been a stumbling block for the Jews (cf. Rm 9–11). But this paradox is "how the mystery is to be dispensed" according to God's plan (3:9).

That God should have chosen as the one to announce the Gospel to the Gentiles a man who "stood out among other Jews of my generation, and how enthusiastic I was for the traditions of my ancestors," who was in fact a persecutor of the Church (Ga 1:13–14) is once more a paradox of the first order. G. K. Chesterton once referred to paradox as the truth standing on its head to draw attention to itself. We know that this message of God's way of making humanity right with him is truly from God, and not merely a projection of our own longings, because it has reversed all our expectations, overturned all that we have perceived as wise, with his powerful foolishness.

The mystery kept hidden from past generations (3:5) and now revealed to the apostles and prophets in the Church is the mystery of God's love, "which is beyond all knowledge" (3:19), but which manifests "how comprehensive God's wisdom really is" (3:10). Human knowledge moves by distinction and separation; human love by preference and selection. But God's love is extended to all, Gentiles as well as Jews: the Gentiles are to "share the same inheritance, be parts of the same body, and receive the same promise" as the Jews (3:6). Gentiles and Jews together can now "approach God in complete confidence" through their shared faith in Christ (3:12). Our human minds cannot really grasp a love so all-inclusive. Even when we have read Paul's way of "explaining how the mystery is to be dispensed" (3:9), we recognize that our knowledge fails. This is why Paul prays (3:16–19) that we might allow our inner selves to be rooted in and grow in the gift of that love. When we accept the gift of God's love for us (which is what is meant by faith, 3:18), this love itself expands within us into a new kind of knowledge; a knowledge which comes from the experience of the Spirit (3:16), the gift of his love within us, and which possesses the power to transform us, to fill us "with the utter fullness of God" (3:19).

The fourth and final paradox is the role of the Church in the revelation of this mystery. Paul has a little play on words in the Greek of 3:14–15, which the *JB* retains in its translation. The Father from whom all things come wishes to draw humans to himself not as disparate individuals, but as a "family" ("father" and "family" are cognate in the Greek). The "family" Paul has in mind is the Church. It is to be the place in the world where the reconciliation between people has effectively taken place. By being truly "family," it manifests to the world that God is truly "father."

What is paradoxical here is not God's desire to bring the Church into existence, but the disparity between the physical stature of the Church in Paul's time and the cosmic role he assigns to it. Paul says that "only now, through the Church" are the cosmic forces to see the all-encompassing wisdom of God (3:10). Paul tells us that the Church does not exist for its own sake alone, but has a function in the world. Before all the forces which resist the fatherhood of God, it is to be a

compelling witness to the unity and love among people
which only God could create. The reconciliation of the
Jews and Gentiles in the one Church is to be the first
and most effective sign of the reconciling power of God
available to all people, indeed all of creation, for he is
the creator of all (3:9).

If the community of faith, the Church, really manifests this unity between people, then it will fulfill its
role in the working out of God's plan "which he had
had from all eternity in Christ Jesus our Lord" (3:11),
and it properly can stand as the place within a divided
world where God's glory can be praised (3:20-21).
But to be Church, the unity must be real, and it is to
this task Paul next turns.

STUDY QUESTION: Does the Church, in your experi-
                ence of it, manifest to the world a
                sign of reconciliation and love?

Ephesians 4:1–16
THE CHURCH AS THE EXPRESSION OF UNITY

¹ I, the prisoner in the Lord, implore you therefore to lead a life worthy of your voca-
² tion. ·Bear with one another charitably, in com-
³ plete selflessness, gentleness and patience. ·Do all you can to preserve the unity of the Spirit by the
⁴ peace that binds you together. ·There is one Body, one Spirit, just as you were all called into one and
⁵ the same hope when you were called. ·There is
⁶ one Lord, one faith, one baptism, ·and one God who is Father of all, over all, through all and within all.

⁷   Each one of us, however, has been given his own share of grace, given as Christ allotted it.
⁸ It was said that he would:

> When he ascended to the height, he captured prisoners,
> he gave gifts to men.

⁹   When it says, "he ascended," what can it mean if not that he descended right down to the lower
¹⁰ regions of the earth? ·The one who rose higher than all the heavens to fill all things is none other

11 than the one who descended. ·And to some, his
gift was that they should be apostles; to some,
prophets; to some, evangelists; to some, pastors
12 and teachers; ·so that the saints together make a
unity in the work of service, building up the
13 body of Christ. ·In this way we are all to come to
unity in our faith and in our knowledge of the
Son of God, until we become the perfect Man,
fully mature with the fullness of Christ himself.
14   Then we shall not be children any longer, or
tossed one way and another and carried along by
every wind of doctrine, at the mercy of all the
tricks men play and their cleverness in practicing
15 deceit. ·If we live by the truth and in love, we
shall grow in all ways into Christ, who is the
16 head ·by whom the whole body is fitted and
joined together, every joint adding its own
strength, for each separate part to work according to its function. So the body grows until it has
built itself up, in love.

✠

Paul begins his formal exhortation to the Ephesians
with this simple point: the first and enduring task of
the Church, the primary way it "leads a life worthy of
its vocation" (4:1) is precisely by *being* the Church.
And if the grace which brought the Church into existence in the first place is a gift of reconciliation between
people and God, and people with each other, then the
vocation of the Church in the world is to manifest this
gift, by being a place where unity and peace can be
found.

The Church is not a social club of like-minded people, whose task is defined by the needs of the members alone; nor is it a cell for social action, whose task is defined by its concrete service to society. The Church is to be the bodying forth in the world of the unifying power of God's love. If it fails to realize that unity within itself, it has failed both its nature and mission.

It is important to see how Paul describes the unity which should be the community's (4:4-13). Is it a kind of uniformity, a denial of difference decreed by discipline or rule? No. It is the unity of life, at once common and diverse, just as the Spirit who gives (and is) that life is at once one in nature and manifold in expression. The basis of Christian unity is a shared experience and conviction. All have the same faith and hope, and have been initiated into the community of this faith and hope by the same baptism (4:5). The common experience is rooted in a common gift: they have all been given new life by the one Spirit, and by it confess together the one Lord who has saved them. Ultimately the unity of Christians is found in the Oneness of God himself from whom comes both gift and call (4:6).

But the other side of the Spirit's gift is equally significant. The diversity within the community is also established by the manifold gifts of the Spirit. These have been given to the community by Christ, who in his death and resurrection obtained sovereignty over every sort of spiritual power and "gave gifts to men" (4:8). Paul cites Ps 68:18 in support of this, making the verse of the Psalm say something quite different than what was intended by the psalmist. For this notion of taking the spiritual forces captive, cf. also Col 2:15.

The spiritual gifts Paul speaks of here are not the

extraordinary manifestations of ecstasy, but the fundamental ministries of service within the community which enable it to "come to unity in our faith and in the knowledge of the Son of God" (4:13). The Apostles, Prophets, Evangelists, Pastors and Teachers all have the gift of addressing the word of the Gospel to the hearts of the community, so that "the body can be built up" (4:16). For this sense of the "edification" of the Church, cf. 1 Co 3:10–15, 14:12. A similar list of ministries is found in Rm 12:3–8, 1 Co 12:28–30. Such ministries do not derive from the desire for dominance, or even from human talent, but from the "share of grace" granted by Christ's Spirit. As Paul says elsewhere, "all these are the work of one and the same spirit who distributes different gifts to different people just as he chooses" (1 Co 12:11; cf. also Heb 2:4, 1 P 4:10–11).

The authentic unity of the Church is not to be sought, then, in rigid conformity, but in rich plurality. The gifts of the Spirit do not destroy the fundamental unity based in God, but reveal how manifold and various God's own life is. The unity of the Church should be an organic unity, like that of a body, whose individual members live by the same life, but express and contribute to that life each within its proper function. It is, therefore, to the image of the body that Paul returns. As with any body, the life which is the Church's must grow. And as the source of its life is the gift of Christ, so is the goal of its growth the full maturity of the body which is "the perfect Man, fully mature with the fullness of Christ himself" (4:13).

There is a condition for this growth, that "we live by the truth and in love" (4:15). The *JB* translation is not quite so strong as the Greek, which says we must "do the truth in love," as though to be truthful and to be loving were one and the same thing. For those whose identity has been established before God by the "word of truth" which is the Gospel, they are the same thing.

This "lived truth" which is the goal of Christian maturity is not stirred by "every wind of doctrine" (4:14), for it is not a truth based first of all in ideas, but in the experience of God's overwhelming love for us in Christ. We have experienced that he is the Head from which the body (whose members we are) gains its growth; and we know that not human cleverness but the expression of love which is his life will be the means by which this body of ours will "build itself up" (4:16).

STUDY QUESTIONS: Can the Church be faithful to its call of manifesting unity in the world when Christians are divided one from another on the basis of doctrine? Is ecumenism just another public relations gambit, or is it a fundamental call to the Church to effectively realize its essential nature?

Ephesians 4:17 – 5:20
THE SPIRITUAL LIFE IS THE LIFE OF
THE SPIRIT

17 In particular, I want to urge you in the name
of the Lord, not to go on living the aimless kind
18 of life that pagans live. ·Intellectually they are in
the dark, and they are estranged from the life of
God, without knowledge because they have shut
19 their hearts to it. ·Their sense of right and wrong
once dulled, they have abandoned themselves to
sexuality and eagerly pursue a career of indecency
20 of every kind. ·Now that is hardly the way you
21 have learned from Christ, ·unless you failed to
hear him properly when you were taught what
22 the truth is in Jesus. ·You must give up your old
way of life; you must put aside your old
self, which gets corrupted by following illusory
23 desires. ·Your mind must be renewed by a spir-
24 itual revolution ·so that you can put on the new
self that has been created in God's way, in the
goodness and holiness of the truth.

25 So from now on, there must be no more lies:
You must speak the truth to one another, since
26 we are all parts of one another. ·Even if you are
angry, you must not sin: never let the sun set on

27 your anger ·or else you will give the devil a foot-
28 hold. ·Anyone who was a thief must stop stealing;
he should try to find some useful manual work
instead, and be able to do some good by helping
29 others that are in need. ·Guard against foul talk;
let your words be for the improvement of others,
as occasion offers, and do good to your listeners,
30 otherwise you will only be grieving the Holy
Spirit of God who has marked you with his seal
for you to be set free when the day comes.
31 Never have grudges against others, or lose your
temper, or raise your voice to anybody, or call
each other names, or allow any sort of spiteful-
32 ness. ·Be friends with one another, and kind, forgiving each other as readily as God forgave you
in Christ.

1 5 Try, then, to imitate God, as children of his
2 that he loves, ·and follow Christ by loving as
he loved you, giving himself up in our place as a
3 fragrant offering and a sacrifice to God. ·Among
you there must be not even a mention of fornication or impurity in any of its forms, or promiscuity: this would hardly become the saints!
4 There must be no coarseness or salacious talk
and jokes—all this is wrong for you; raise your
5 voices in thanksgiving instead. ·For you can be
quite certain that nobody who actually indulges
in fornication or impurity or promiscuity—which
is worshiping a false god—can inherit anything of
6 the kingdom of God. ·Do not let anyone deceive
you with empty arguments: it is for this loose
living that God's anger comes down on those
7 who rebel against him. ·Make sure that you are
8 not included with them. ·You were darkness once,
but now you are light in the Lord; be like children
9 of light, ·for the effects of the light are seen in
complete goodness and right living and truth.
10 Try to discover what the Lord wants of you,
11 having nothing to do with the futile works of

¹² darkness but exposing them by contrast. ·The
things which are done in secret are things that
¹³ people are ashamed even to speak of; ·but anything exposed by the light will be illuminated
¹⁴ and anything illuminated turns into light. That is
why it is said:

> Wake up from your sleep,
> rise from the dead,
> and Christ will shine on you.

¹⁵ So be very careful about the sort of lives you lead,
like intelligent and not like senseless people.
¹⁶ This may be a wicked age, but your lives should
¹⁷ redeem it. ·And do not be thoughtless but recog-
¹⁸ nize what is the will of the Lord. ·Do not drug
yourselves with wine; this is simply dissipation;
¹⁹ be filled with the Spirit. ·Sing the words and tunes
of the psalms and hymns when you are together,
and go on singing and chanting to the Lord in
²⁰ your hearts, ·so that always and everywhere you
are giving thanks to God who is our Father in
the name of our Lord Jesus Christ.

☩

If the Church is to manifest to a divided world that
God wills for humanity a new form of unity, based not
on human congeniality but on the gift of the Holy
Spirit, then the life of the community must breathe by
this Spirit. The members are to be "filled with the Holy
Spirit" (5:18); they are not to "grieve the Holy Spirit
of God who has marked you with his seal" (4:30);
they are to allow their minds to be "renewed by a spiritual revolution" (4:23). This renewal of their minds is
basic. Paul knows that human behavior flows from and
expresses our fundamental attitudes and perceptions. If

these are not transformed, there will be no real change in behavior; even what appears to be "piety" can, in truth, be a subtle form of selfishness.

So, he contrasts the attitudes of the past and the present. Formerly, they had shut their hearts to the knowledge of God, with the result that their perception of themselves, the world, and God, had become distorted. They had been as those stumbling in the darkness (4:18), who were so separated from light they did not even know to call it "darkness," but thought it to be "reality." From this distorted view came all their wicked behavior (4:19, 5:3–5). Now, says Paul, they must allow the Spirit to act upon them in shaping a whole new attitude. They are to "put aside" that old self (4:22) and "put on the new self which has been created in God's way, in the goodness and holiness of the truth" (4:24). In this clothing metaphor, as in the light/darkness imagery which follows, we again find traces of the primitive Christian baptismal language. Paul says the new self is to be characterized by holiness and truth. The two terms are closely connected, just as love and truth were, earlier (4:15).

The community is to be holy. Israel had been called to be a "holy nation" for the Lord (Ex 19:6), and was told, "you shall be holy, for I, the Lord your God, am holy" (Lv 19:2). The call to holiness is the call to be different in the world because of belief in the One God. In Judaism, this "difference" came to be identified with the keeping of certain laws, and the ritual "holiness" of the Jews only served to sharpen the alienation between peoples. The holiness of the Christian community is not to be found in the observance of law or ritual, but in obedience to the Spirit of God, precisely through the

renewal of Christians' hearts and minds. Christians
have a new standard of holiness: they are to "imitate
God" (5:1), by following the example of love he revealed to them in Christ, "who gave himself in our
place" (5:2, cf. Ga 1:4). Israel's call to holiness has
not been abrogated; it has been fulfilled in that outpouring of God's love upon Jews and Gentiles alike in
the Church, which has created a new people.

No more than the kingdom which was Israel can the
"kingdom of God" be corrupted by any form of idolatry or perversion (5:3–6; cf. 1 Co 6:9–11). But the
true standard of Christian holiness is not legalism
which stands in judgment on the neighbor. It is, rather,
that loving forgiveness toward each other shown first to
us in Christ: "Be friends with one another, and kind,
forgiving each other as readily as God forgave you in
Christ" (4:32).

To be holy is to be different. And there is a real
sense in which the life of the Christian community
should set it in contrast to the attitudes and behavior of
that part of the world (and it is a part within each of
us as well) which resists the call of God and does not
wish to find in him its standard of measurement. Paul
uses the images of light and darkness for this contrast
(5:9–15). So great has been the illumination of their
lives through the experience of Christ (5:14), it is possible to see both their former lives and the lives of
others as being in "darkness," and themselves now as
"children of light" (5:8). It is not appropriate for
those in the light to share in the evil deeds of those in
the darkness (5:12; cf. Rm 13:11–14, 1 Th 5:4–11, 2
Co 6:14–18).

But Paul does *not* say that Christians are to reject

those outside the community as evil, or show hostility toward them. To live by different standards is not a warrant for a smug sectarianism. On the contrary, their lives are to be so suffused with the light of Christ that they have a positive influence on those outside. They can "expose the works of darkness by contrast" (5:12), by providing a real alternative in the world to the futility of evil. Paul is confident that "anything exposed by the light will be illuminated and anything illuminated turns into light" (5:14). Christians are not to hide their light under a basket, but place it on a stand, "for there is nothing hidden but it must be disclosed, nothing kept secret except to be brought to light" (Mk 4:21–22). Christians are not to turn away from the world in condemnation, but turn toward it in love: "This may be a wicked age, but your lives should redeem it" (5:16).

The Church is to be a community of truth. It has been called into existence by the "word of truth" which is the Gospel (1:13). The enlightenment of believers has led them to recognize the truth about God and his way of bringing humans into union with him and with each other. They have been taught "what the truth is in Jesus" (4:21). If the Church is to be true to its identity, it must be the place in the world where the truth is to be found. And this is not first of all a matter of proper doctrine. There is no question this is important, for the right understanding of the gift is a necessary framework for the living out of the gift, and Paul rejects any false teaching as dangerous (4:21,14–15, 5:6). But the truth they have learned in Jesus is above all a lived truth, a matter of perception, attitude and action.

The kind of truthfulness Paul emphasizes here is the truth of relationships within the community. In 4:15, he said that we are to do the truth in love. Here, he spells out what that means. There is a striking stress placed on the truthfulness of speech, for speech is the first of our symbols, and where it is distorted, relationships get skewed. As the sexual life of Christians should be marked by reverence and care, so should speech about sex: "There must be no coarseness or salacious talk and jokes—all this is wrong for you" (5:5). A seemingly harmless risqué remark may reveal a distorted perception of the holiness of relations between male and female.

At a deeper level, still, speech is to be truthful. Christians are not to lie, but "you must speak the truth to one another" (4:25). We notice that this statement comes right before, "Even if you are angry, you must not sin." Paul cites here Ps 4:4, and it is difficult to discover exactly what he intends by it. He says that the sun should not set on our anger. What is important to note here, is that Paul does not deny the reality of human anger. It is a part of life, and indeed, a part of the truth about relations between humans.

Anger is the most difficult of all virtues to learn. Much of Christian piety has been built on the denial of anger. And this is a form of falsehood. Anger between people is dangerous and harmful only when "the sun sets on it," that is, when anger is allowed to build and fester within us, and turn to hostility. When anger becomes hostility, "the devil gets a foothold" (4:27). The truth is done in love, when Christians learn to express anger in healthy and appropriate ways, and not, through some perverse ideal of passive virtue, allow suppressed anger to become devastating hostility, the kind which "holds grudges" (4:31).

There is more to "speaking the truth to each other" than avoiding lies. Just as the thief is to stop stealing, and is to work so that others can be helped (4:28), so should speech have the positive effect of helping the needs of others, "building them up" in their faith (4:29; the *JB* has "be for the improvement"). Just as the ministries of the word within the community serve to "build up" the Church, so should the speech between members of the community. This has less to do with pious jargon and dropping references to God into conversation, than with the simple but difficult ideal of speaking truthfully to others. When the relations between Christians are characterized by such truthfulness in deed and speech, then the psalms and hymns of Christian worship will be an authentic expression before God of the actual life of the Church, which is "always and everywhere giving thanks to God who is our Father in the name of our Lord Jesus Christ" (5:19–20).

STUDY QUESTIONS: How can the Church encourage the "doing of truth in love" among its members? How have we come to regard anger as opposed to love, rather than its expression? Is there a place for "loving dissent" within the Church?

Ephesians 5:21 – 6:9
NORMS FOR CHRISTIAN HOUSEHOLDS

21 Give way to one another in obedience to Christ.
22 Wives should regard their husbands as they re-
23 gard the Lord, ·since as Christ is head of the
Church and saves the whole body, so is a hus-
24 band the head of his wife; ·and as the Church
submits to Christ, so should wives to their hus-
25 bands, in everything. ·Husbands should love their
wives just as Christ loved the Church and sac-
26 rificed himself for her ·to make her holy. He
made her clean by washing her in water with a
27 form of words, ·so that when he took her to himself she would be glorious, with no speck or
wrinkle or anything like that, but holy and fault-
28 less. ·In the same way, husbands must love their
wives as they love their own bodies; for a man to
29 love his wife is for him to love himself. ·A man
never hates his own body, but he feeds it and
looks after it; and that is the way Christ treats
30 the Church, ·because it is his body—and we are its
31 living parts. ·For this reason, a man must leave
his father and mother and be joined to his wife,
32 and the two will become one body. ·This mystery

has many implications; but I am saying it applies
33 to Christ and the Church. ·To sum up; you too, each one of you, must love his wife as he loves himself; and let every wife respect her husband.

1 6 Children, be obedient to your parents in the
2   Lord—that is your duty. ·The first command-ment that has a promise attached to it is: Honor
3 your father and mother, ·and the promise is: and you will prosper and have a long life in the land.
4 And parents, never drive your children to resent-ment but in bringing them up correct them and guide them as the Lord does.

5   Slaves, be obedient to the men who are called your masters in this world, with deep respect and
6 sincere loyalty, as you are obedient to Christ: ·not only when you are under their eye, as if you had only to please men, but because you are slaves of Christ and wholeheartedly do the will
7 of God. ·Work hard and willingly, but do it for the sake of the Lord and not for the sake of
8 men. ·You can be sure that everyone, whether a slave or a free man, will be properly rewarded by the Lord for whatever work he has done well.
9 And those of you who are employers, treat your slaves in the same spirit; do without threats, re-membering that they and you have the same Mas-ter in heaven and he is not impressed by one per-son more than by another.

✝

Paul makes the transition to the special obligations of those living together in households with this general command: "Give way to one another in obedience to Christ" (5:21). In the Christian community, not only those at the lower end of power arrangements are to be

submissive; everyone is called to demonstrate this attitude of "selflessness, gentleness and patience" (4:2).

For a general introduction to these household instructions and the difficulties they present, the reader
can refer to the commentary on Col 3:18 – 4:1. Concerning the relations between slaves and masters, parents and children, Paul's instructions here are virtually
identical to the ones there. Again, there is no condemnation of slavery, but a mitigation of its effect, by the
emphasis on obedience directed to the Lord, and by the
recognition that slave owners, too, "have the same
Master in heaven and he is not impressed by one person more than by another" (6:8–9). As in Col 3:20,
children are ordered to show obedience and honor to
their parents (6:1–4). It is striking that Paul here
quotes the Scripture (Ex 20:12) and notes that this is
a command which carries with it a blessing. Striking,
because the Old Testament is very rarely cited in Ephesians (five times in all). By means of the citation, Paul
makes it clear that *both* mother and father are to be
shown honor by the children. As everywhere in that
culture, it was the father's responsibility to "correct
and guide" the children (that is, educate them), but
this passage places parents of both sexes in a position
of equal respect in the eyes of children.

Certainly the most beautiful and troublesome part of
this passage is that dealing with the relations between
man and woman in marriage. There is perhaps no text
of Scripture which has occasioned so many tears of joy
at weddings and so many tears of bitterness later. It is
a text susceptible to distortion. It would be a distortion
for either husband or wife to deny the legitimate
growth in our understanding of the equality of the

sexes before God (an understanding rooted ultimately in Paul's own thought), and use this text either to assert the total domination of the husband over the life of the woman, or the passive refusal of a woman to accept responsibility for her own life before God.

For the woman to regard her husband as "the head" as the Church sees Christ as its head (5:23; cf. also 1 Co 11:3) no more relieves a woman from responsibility for her own life and the life of her family, than the Church is relieved from the responsibility of exercising the "freedom of the sons of God" (Rm 8:21). Once this is said, however, it must be recognized that Paul here sees the woman as being obedient to her husband in a way the husband is not to her. This is a difficulty for us. And there is no easy answer. To throw out the Scripture because it does not match our own perception would be a betrayal. Equally great a betrayal would be the denial of our perception in favor of this culturally conditioned norm. Somehow, we must exist in the tension created by the distance between this norm and our experience. Part of the importance of reading such "stumbling block" passages is that they remind us that our perceptions, too, are culturally conditioned, as are our forms of family and social life. It is not necessary to choose one over the other. It is necessary to listen to the truth each one expresses, as we grow from one stage to another. One truth we can learn is that there is, inevitably and rightly, structure to every social grouping, and within this structure, place for authority. Seeing the sort of attitudes Paul wished Christians within another authority structure to have helps us to discern the sort of attitudes we ought to have within ours.

Because what Paul has to say clashes so strongly with our perception of the mutual roles of men and women, we can easily miss the importance of what he says to husbands, at whom his remarks are primarily directed. If the woman is to be submissive to the man within marriage (note, this itself is not an absolute statement of submission to every man by every woman), the husband is to show submission to the wife in an even profounder sense. His attitude of love toward his wife is to be that of Christ toward the Church, who "sacrificed himself for her to make her holy" (5:25). But the sanctification is not all one way; Paul says in another place that the husband can be sanctified through the example of the wife (1 Co 7:14).

Paul sees the unity between husband and wife in marriage as so profound that it approximates the unity between Christ and the Church: it is a unity of life and of love, which makes two persons "one body." And the particular responsibility Paul assigns to the husband is the sort of love which leads him to leave all other relationships and "become one body" with his wife (5:29–31).

The most important aspect of this whole passage is the positive role it assigns to marriage. This represents a real progression from Paul's thought in 1 Corinthians 7. There, marriage was seen as a legitimate state for Christians, but in the light of the tribulations Paul then thought shortly to come, less desirable than virginity. Here, on the other hand, we find a vision of marriage which is entirely positive. Paul calls it a "great mystery" and refers it directly to the mystery of Christ and the Church (5:32). In Ephesians, Paul sees the Church as that place in the world where the reconciliation between God and humans is expressed in the reconciliation between persons. The role he assigns to marriage is to be that vocation within the Church, the ministry of husband and wife together, which expresses in the most concrete form that this unity is real. It is an awesome vocation.

STUDY QUESTIONS: Has the sense of marriage as a real "vocation" within the Church been a living part of the Christian consciousness? How can husbands and wives "sanctify" each other and their children?

Ephesians 6:10–24
SPIRITUAL WARFARE WITH WEAPONS
OF PEACE

10 Finally, grow strong in the Lord, with the
11 strength of his power. ·Put God's armor on so as
12 to be able to resist the devil's tactics. ·For it is
not against human enemies that we have to struggle, but against the Sovereignties and the Powers who originate the darkness in this world, the
13 spiritual army of evil in the heavens. ·That is why
you must rely on God's armor, or you will not
be able to put up any resistance when the worst
happens, or have enough resources to hold your
ground.
14 So stand your ground, with truth buckled
around your waist, and integrity for a breast-
15 plate, ·wearing for shoes on your feet the eager-
16 ness to spread the gospel of peace ·and always
carrying the shield of faith so that you can use
it to put out the burning arrows of the evil one.
17 And then you must accept salvation from God
to be your helmet and receive the word of God
from the Spirit to use as a sword.
18 Pray all the time, asking for what you need,
praying in the Spirit on every possible occasion.

Never get tired of staying awake to pray for all
19 the saints; ·and pray for me to be given an opportunity to open my mouth and speak without
20 fear and give out the mystery of the gospel ·of
which I am an ambassador in chains; pray that
in proclaiming it I may speak as boldly as I
ought to.
21   I should like you to know, as well, what is
happening to me and what I am doing; my dear
brother Tychicus, my loyal helper in the Lord,
22 will tell you everything. ·I am sending him to
you precisely for this purpose, to give you news
about us and reassure you.
23   May God the Father and the Lord Jesus Christ
grant peace, love and faith to all the brothers.
24 May grace and eternal life be with all who love
our Lord Jesus Christ.

✠

There is an almost shocking shift in tone in these
final exhortations. Paul's common-sense directives concerning behavior in the household give way to a highly
colored imagery of warfare on the cosmic scale. The
military language is particularly surprising in a letter
which has so stressed the peace which has come to the
world as a result of the work of Christ. What is happening here?

Paul is simply reminding his readers that the peace
won for them in Christ is one which exists in a divided
world; that the Church cannot rest comfortably within
this peace, but must make it real within the world; and
that there are forces at work in the world which resist

God's call to peace. Earlier, he had said that the mystery had been hidden, "so that the Sovereignties and Powers should learn only now, through the Church, how comprehensive God's wisdom really is" (3:10). Behind the history of human struggle in the world, Paul sees a more basic warfare. Behind the Church, he sees the power of God at work; and behind all the organized and systematized forms of evil rule and government in the world, he sees the influence of the evil angelic powers. Paul does not see all the evil in the world as the work simply of "flesh and blood," but as stemming from a deeper, more spiritual force. The seductive wiles of systemic corruption are the "devil's tactics." Paul's language may be mythological, but the reality he points to is frightening enough, for we have all experienced the appalling force of evil, not just in individuals, but in the kind of collective evil which can seize individuals and become virtually cosmic in power. The Nazi atrocities and the Soviet Gulag Archipelago are two examples from our own generation of systemic evil on a scale we can scarcely grasp.

Against such organized evildoing, the good will and effort of individuals is not sufficient. The only power equal to this is the power of God. That is why Paul prays that we "grow strong in the Lord, with the strength of his power" (6:10; cf. also Ph 4:13, 1 Tm 1:12, 2 Tm 2:1). The imagery of spiritual armor seems to be traditional. We find it used in the Qumran documents, and Paul employs it elsewhere (Rm 13:12,14, 2 Co 6:7, 10:4, 1 Th 5:8), but never so elaborately as here. Paul is not issuing a call to some sort of Christian crusade or militant fanaticism. The armament is not for attack, but for defense, to enable the Christians to "resist the evil one" (cf. Jm 4:7, 1 P 5:9). Since the struggle is not against other people, the weapons are not material weapons. The battle is spiritual, and the armament must be those spiritual qualities with which the Christians are already clothed when they put on the Lord Jesus (cf. Rm 13:14) at baptism. Paul's call to them is that they activate these qualities in their lives. That this is the case can be seen from the Old Testament texts Paul weaves together in elaborating this allegorical armor. The qualities of "truth," of "integrity," and the "helmet of salvation" come from two passages of Isaiah (11:5 and 59:17), which describe, respectively, the qualities of the Messiah and of God himself. The Christians are to recognize, in the face of continuing and seemingly unconquerable evil in the world, that the power of overcoming this evil lies not within them, but with the power which comes from God. To the extent they allow this power to be at work in their lives will they "have enough resources to hold your ground" (6:13). The truth, the integrity, the faith are not works of human achievement, but gifts from God. His is the "Gospel of peace," his the "sword of the Spirit." For this reason, Paul appropriately ends the letter by telling his readers to place themselves in the posture of people waiting upon the Lord: "Pray all the time, asking for what you need, praying in the Spirit on every possible occasion" (6:18). They are to pray, not only for themselves, but "for all the saints," knowing that they are praying to "him whose power, working in us, can do infinitely more than we can ask or imagine; glory be to him from generation to generation in the

Church and in Christ Jesus for ever and ever. Amen" (3:20–21).

STUDY QUESTION: Do we do justice to the reality of evil in the world when we see it simply as the result of individual vice or sickness?

The Pastoral Epistles
Letters to Paul's Co-Workers

Paul's letters to his co-workers Timothy and Titus have a special place within the Pauline collection, and a few words of introduction on their special character may be helpful.

Paul's correspondence with his communities was of an occasional nature. He liked to deal with problems at first hand and frequently was frustrated at having to deal with them by letter. When he wrote, it was because there was some problem in a Church, or some personal project, which needed attention, even at a distance.

Because each letter was written for a specific purpose, each is marked by the sort of problems addressed. In none of them do we find all of Paul's teaching. There is a shift in emphasis from letter to letter, just as we would expect in a real correspondence. The Thessalonian Church was bothered by the question of Christ's coming; Paul says nothing to them of justification by faith. In Galatians and Colossians, where the crisis has to do with the keeping of the Law of Moses, little is said about the second coming. To the Corinthians, whose spiritual gifts are disrupting community worship, Paul talks a great deal more about the role of the Spirit in the community, than he does to the Colossians. And so forth.

There are, of course, certain convictions and themes running through all these letters which we can identify as Pauline: his awareness of his special apostolic commission, his conviction that we are saved not by our own efforts but by God's grace, his emphasis on the death and resurrection of Jesus the Messiah, and the pivotal importance of faith as the response to the Gospel message, his concern for love and good order within the Church.

If the needs of individual communities affected the tone and topics of Paul's letters to them, we would naturally expect letters written to fellow workers to be marked by distinctive concerns. And such is the case. With the partial exception of Philemon, these are the only letters of Paul still in our possession which were written not to communities but to individuals; and not to just any individuals, but to two of his most trusted delegates.

From Paul's other letters and from the Acts of the Apostles, we learn something of the role men like Timothy and Titus played in the Pauline mission. It was a critical one. They were more than casual helpers. They were men of substance, genuine collaborators in the mission; under Paul's direction, to be sure, but with a real share in responsibility: preachers, teachers and administrators in their own right.

Timothy was one of Paul's closest associates. He was intimately involved with Paul's work for the Thessalonian and Philippian churches. He cosponsored with Paul several of the major letters (cf. 2 Co 1:1, Ph 1:1, Col 1:1, 1 and 2 Th 1:1, Phm 1), and appears in the final greetings of Rm 16:21. Timothy was sent by Paul to the Corinthians to "remind you of the way that I live in Christ, as I teach it everywhere in all the churches (1 Co 4:17), and Paul wishes "no one to be scornful of him" (1 Co 16:10–11). Timothy took part with Paul in the initial preaching of the Gospel to the Corinthians (2 Co 1:19). Paul tells the Philippians, "I hope, in the Lord Jesus, to send Timothy to you soon. . . . I have no one like him here, as wholeheartedly concerned for your welfare" (Ph 2:19). And when he could no longer bear to be away from the Thessalonians, Paul sent Timothy "our brother and God's servant in the Gospel of Christ, to establish you in your faith and to exhort you" (1 Th 3:2).

We know less about Titus. He was a Greek believer who accompanied Paul to Jerusalem, and whom Paul would not allow to be circumcised (Ga 2:1–3). He seems to have worked closely with Paul especially in the Corinthian Church (2 Co 2:13, 7:6,13) and was Paul's emissary to that community in the period of the Corinthian correspondence. He was given charge of the collection in Corinth (2 Co 8:6), and Paul calls him "my partner and fellow worker in your service" (2 Co 8:23).

What would we expect Paul's concerns to be in letters written to such men, whose role it was to represent him in various churches, to "remind" them of Paul's teaching, and "to establish them in their faith and exhort them"?

We would expect just the sort of attention to organization not appropriate in letters written to communities at large. We would expect advice on the ordering of communities, and the qualities expected of leaders. We would not be surprised to find a stress placed on correct teaching as one of these qualities, nor a certain harshness exhibited toward those who were insinuating themselves into churches as opposing teachers and whose personal ambitions both distorted the message they taught and threatened the stability of churches. Above all, we would expect a considerable amount of encouragement and personal exhortation from Paul to his delegates, since their work among the refractory Pauline churches was often thankless. These are precisely the sorts of concerns we find in the Pastoral Letters.

The special character of the Pastorals is found in the central focus of all three letters: the attitudes and practices of Paul's delegates as teachers. Paul had no need to give them detailed instruction in the faith, or to correct their errors; they were his trusted helpers. But he did feel the need to remind them of the demands of their task as teachers. He wanted to refresh their spirit by recalling to their minds the basis of their call and its exigencies.

In Paul's time, there was a definite literary form for a letter such as this. It was called a paraenetic letter. Paraenesis is a kind of ethical instruction which is concerned not with new, but traditional teaching: that which was already known but needed reminding. A letter of paraenesis was written in order to remind someone of his/her duties. An important part of the letter was the presentation of a concrete model for imitation. In the Pastorals, as we might expect, Paul presents himself as the model to Timothy and Titus. He wants them, in turn, to be models for their own communities. It was understood that true virtue could be learned only from its exemplification in a human life.

In the typical paraenetic letter, this model was expanded by means of concrete directives: do this, and avoid that. In the Pastorals, we find these directives too, but given a distinct tone by the interest Paul has in the teaching role of his delegates. What are they to avoid? The false teachings of the heretics, and above all their methods and motives. What are they to imitate? The healthy teaching of Paul, and his attitudes of patience, gentleness and endurance. Paul uses this literary form (as he did that of the diatribe in Romans) with great flexibility. 2 Timothy is an almost purely personal paraenetic letter, and we will read it first, to see how it forms the framework for understanding the other two letters. In 1 Timothy and Titus, Paul inserts practical directives concerning the order of the community within the framework of the personal paraenetic letter, but his focus on the mission and attitudes of his delegates remains constant.

Many readers have been struck by the moralistic tone of these letters, and by how much more Greek they sound than, say, Galatians or Romans. This is partly due to the fact that Paul is writing to men whose education was undoubtedly Greek. But it may owe more to the form and function of the letters themselves. Timothy and Titus are being addressed as teachers. The kind of attitudes held by the best of the

teachers in Greek culture are here recommended to
Paul's delegates. As the true philosopher (that is,
moral teacher) of Paul's day was to be at once severe
and gentle, patient and aggressive, like a physician of
souls, so are these Christian teachers to be like physi-
cians of souls, teaching sound and healthy doctrine,
eschewing the sickness of corrupt ideas. The difference
is that the healthy teaching Paul recommends has not
to do with the asceticism of the sage, but with the saving message of the Gospel, "that Christ Jesus came
into the world to save sinners" (1 Tm 1:15).

2 Timothy
"God's Word Cannot Be Bound"

Paul wrote the second letter to Timothy from prison (1:8, 2:9), probably in Rome (1:17). He had apparently completed a first defense before the authorities (4:16). Although he feels alone and abandoned (1:15, 4:16), he has about him several helpers (4:11,21), is receiving visitors (1:16–17), and is in touch with the movements of his co-workers (4:10,12,19–20). There is a mood of finality and resignation in this letter; Paul is facing the probability of his defense failing and himself being killed. He speaks of his end being near (4:6–8). His mood is similar to that in Philippians 1:21–26. But there, he hoped to be freed and returned to his community (Ph 1:26); here, he has no such earthly confidence. His hope is in the Lord delivering him from every evil work and bringing him safely into his heavenly kingdom (4:18). Faced with such personal discouragement, he is the more eager to encourage his most intimate co-worker, Timothy, to "stand fast" in his proclamation of the Gospel, even when experiencing rejection and opposition (4:1–5).

Paul's whole concern in this personal letter is to strengthen Timothy's courage and commitment, for it is clear that Timothy, too, is discouraged (1:6–8). He uses the form of the paraenetic letter to remind Timothy of his calling; the purpose of the reminder is to stir to new enthusiasm and commitment (1:6). In the first part of the letter, Paul presents himself to Timothy as the model of preaching the Gospel and suffering for it. In the second part of the letter, Paul presents to Timothy the ideal attitudes and practices of the Christian preacher and teacher, by means of constant contrast to the false teachers who were giving Timothy such trouble (2:14 – 4:5). At the end, he returns to himself as model (4:6–8), and to final practical instructions.

Some have suggested that 2 Timothy is Paul's "farewell discourse" or "last testament." Paul (or, if the letter was pseudonymously written, his disciples) may have so intended it to be read. In any case, this small letter's significance reaches well beyond its original purpose, and reminds all those who wish to bear witness to the Lord through word and action that, in spite of all the frustration and suffering endemic to such a vocation, "God's word cannot be bound" (2:9).

2 Timothy 1:1–14
REKINDLING THE GIFT OF GOD

1 From Paul, appointed by God to be an apostle of Christ Jesus in his design to promise
2 life in Christ Jesus; ·to Timothy, dear child of mine, wishing you grace, mercy and peace from God the Father and from Christ Jesus our Lord.
3 Night and day I thank God, keeping my conscience clear and remembering my duty to him as my ancestors did, and always I remember you
4 in my prayers; I remember your tears ·and long
5 to see you again to complete my happiness. ·Then I am reminded of the sincere faith which you have; it came first to live in your grandmother Lois, and your mother Eunice, and I have no doubt that it is the same faith in you as well.
6 This is why I am reminding you now to fan into a flame the gift that God gave you when I
7 laid my hands on you. ·God's gift was not a spirit of timidity, but the Spirit of power and love and
8 self-control. ·So you are never to be ashamed of witnessing to the Lord or ashamed of me for being his prisoner; but with me bear the hardships for the sake of the Good News, relying on the power

⁹ of God ·who has saved us and called us to be
holy—not because of anything we ourselves have
done but for his own purpose and by his own
grace. This grace had already been granted to us,
¹⁰ in Christ Jesus, before the beginning of time, ·but
it has only been revealed by the Appearing of
our Savior Christ Jesus. He abolished death, and
he has proclaimed life and immortality through
¹¹ the Good News; ·and I have been named its herald, its apostle and its teacher.

¹² It is only on account of this that I am experiencing fresh hardships here now; but I have not
lost confidence, because I know who it is that I
have put my trust in, and I have no doubt at all
that he is able to take care of all that I have
entrusted to him until that Day.

¹³ Keep as your pattern the sound teaching you
have heard from me, in the faith and love that
¹⁴ are in Christ Jesus. ·You have been trusted to
look after something precious; guard it with the
help of the Holy Spirit who lives in us.

✠

The warm personal tone of this letter is evident from
the beginning. Paul addresses Timothy as "dear child
of mine" (1:2; cf. Ph 2:22). His thanksgiving is de-
voted to the memory of Timothy's faith, and that of his
maternal forebears, Lois and Eunice (1:5). Timothy's
father was a Greek unbeliever (Ac 16:1–3), and he
learned his "sincere faith" from his mother and grandmother. Ordinarily in this kind of letter, mention would
be made of the moral training received from the father,
who in that world was responsible for the education of

sons. It is striking testimony to the influence of these
women in Timothy's life that Paul gives them such attention here.

In his prayer, Paul "remembers" Timothy (1:3), he
"remembers" his tears (1:4), he "remembers" his sincere faith (1:5). This emphasis on memory is characteristic of paraenetic letters. What kind of memory is
it? Certainly not mechanical recall of information from
the past. It is, rather, an act of spiritual fidelity, in
which the heart allows the past and the absent to become present in a living and powerful way. Such memory is a form of spiritual communion, and is an essential aspect of prayer. It is because Paul remembers
Timothy in this way that he can "remind" Timothy,
that is, make alive again for him, his own example
(1:6).

Timothy is discouraged. This is clear not only from
Paul's mention of his tears (1:4), but also from the
hesitant tone of "and I have no doubt that it is the
same faith in you as well" (1:5). Timothy's courage
has been sapped, he has grown timid in his work as a
preacher because of the severe opposition he encoun-
ters. He may even be feeling some shame, not only because of what he has had to suffer because of the Gospel, but especially because his own teacher, Paul, is
imprisoned.

Paul's exhortation is directed to this discouragement
and shame. He reminds Timothy to "fan into a flame
the gift that God gave you when I laid my hands on
you" (1:6). This "laying on of hands" refers to the act
of appointing ministers in the New Testament (cf. e.g.
Ac 13:1–3), which was seen as a real empowerment by
the Holy Spirit (cf. Ac 6:6, 14:23, 1 Tm 4:14). The

Spirit so given was not one of "timidity" but precisely one of power to proclaim the Gospel (cf. Lk 4:14, 24:49, Ac 1:8, 6:8, 19:11, 1 Co 2:4, 2 Co 12:12, 1 Th 1:5). It is this Spirit Paul wishes to breathe to living flame in Timothy.

Strengthened by this Spirit, Timothy need not be ashamed, either of bearing witness to the Lord, or of the sufferings experienced by Paul. He will be able to "bear the hardships" with Paul for the sake of the Gospel, relying not on his own power, but "on the power of God" (1:8). Paul tells Timothy that "you have been trusted to look after something precious; guard it with the help of the Holy Spirit who lives in us" (1:14). What model does Timothy have to follow in all of this? Paul himself. Paul is a model, first of all, of sound teaching, and of the attitudes of "faith and love in Christ Jesus" (1:13). But more than that, he is the model of suffering without shame for the Gospel, and guarding to the end the precious deposit which is the Gospel (1:12). Paul is able to endure in his suffering because *he* has placed his trust in the power of God, just as he has told Timothy to do (1:12).

Paul's language concerning his call and the Gospel he preaches (1:8–11) contains an intriguing mixture of typical Pauline elements and new formulations. It is characteristic of Paul to attach a short summary of the Gospel message to statements about his special apostolic call (cf. Rm 1:1–6, 1 Co 15:3–10, Ga 1:1–4, Ph 3:4–11). The emphasis here on the power of God at work in the Gospel to save recalls Rm 1:16–17, 1 Co 1:18. The sharp contrast between grace and human works, and the note of eternal predestination, recall Rm 8:28–30, Ep 1:4–14, 2:8–10. The description of

Christ's saving act as a destruction of death and a "shining forth" of life resembles the language of Colossians and Ephesians (for "immortality" and the resurrection life, cf. 1 Co 15:42–43).

On the other hand, there is language here which is found in all three Pastorals, but only rarely or not at all in Paul's other letters. For example, Paul here calls Jesus Christ "our Savior," which is elsewhere used of Jesus only in Ph 3:20 and Ep 5:23. "Apostle" is, together with "servant," one of Paul's favorite self-designations. But here, he calls himself as well "herald" and "teacher" (1:11). Finally, although the transmission of the Gospel by means of tradition is, of course, very much a part of Paul's understanding elsewhere (cf. 1 Co 11:2, 15:3–8, 2 Th 2:15), he here uses an expression, "something precious" (Greek: "deposit"), for the tradition, which is found only in the Pastorals. Together with the command to "guard it," this description seems to indicate less a living development of tradition than the preservation of what has already been handed down.

STUDY QUESTION: Compare the opening of this letter to the beginning of the Letter to Philemon. How is Paul's personal affection for Timothy manifested here?

2 Timothy 1:15 – 2:13
TIMOTHY'S MODELS

15 As you know, Phygelus and Hermogenes and all the others from Asia refuse to have anything 16 more to do with me. ·I hope the Lord will be kind to all the family of Onesiphorus, because he has often been a comfort to me and has never 17 been ashamed of my chains. ·On the contrary, as soon as he reached Rome, he really searched 18 hard for me and found·out where I was. ·May it be the Lord's will that he shall find the Lord's mercy on that Day. You know better than anyone else how much he helped me at Ephesus.

1 2 Accept the strength, my dear son, that comes
2 from the grace of Christ Jesus. ·You have heard everything that I teach in public; hand it on to reliable people so that they in turn will be able to teach others.

3 Put up with your share of difficulties, like a
4 good soldier of Christ Jesus. ·In the army, no soldier gets himself mixed up in civilian life, because he must be at the disposal of the man who
5 enlisted him; ·or take an athlete—he cannot win

any crown unless he has kept all the rules of the
6 contest; ·and again, it is the working farmer who
has the first claim on any crop that is harvested.
7 Think over what I have said, and the Lord will
show you how to understand it all.
8   Remember the Good News that I carry, "Jesus Christ risen from the dead, sprung from the
9 race of David"; ·it is on account of this that I
have my own hardships to bear, even to being
chained like a criminal—but they cannot chain up
10 God's news. ·So I bear it all for the sake of those
who are chosen, so that in the end they may have
the salvation that is in Christ Jesus and the
eternal glory that comes with it.
11 Here is a saying that you can rely on:

If we have died with him, then we shall live
    with him.
12 If we hold firm, then we shall reign with him.
If we disown him, then he will disown us.
13 We may be unfaithful, but he is always faithful,
for he cannot disown his own self.

✠

Paul's remarks about Onesiphorus in 1:15–18 may
eem strange, until we recognize that Paul is presenting
im to Timothy as a model. We have seen that Paul
vants Timothy to have courage and not to be ashamed
f Paul's suffering. The clear inference we draw from
1e refusal of Phygelus, Hermogenes and others of
sia "to have anything more to do with me" (1:15) is
1at they abandoned Paul out of shame caused by his
nprisonment. But Onesiphorus "has never been
shamed of my chains" (1:16), and expended great

effort to seek Paul out in prison and find him. There is
a fine play on words in the Greek, retained by the *JB*
translation: Onesiphorus "found" Paul; Paul, in turn,
prays that in the day of judgment he will "find" mercy
from the Lord (1:17–18). Onesiphorus' attitude and
action should stand as an example to Timothy, whom
Paul has told, "do not be ashamed," and in 4:9, tells,
"do your best to come and see me as soon as you can."

Paul returns in 2:1 to his explicit exhortation. Timothy is himself to "accept the strength" that comes
from the grace of Christ Jesus. We understand here a
reference to that Holy Spirit of power which enables
Timothy to proclaim the Gospel and suffer for its sake
(1:7,14). Timothy is also to hand on the teachings he
received from Paul to other reliable teachers (2:2).
The responsibility of Paul's delegates for the con-
tinuance of authentic teaching through the appointment
of others is developed explicitly in 1 Timothy and
Titus, but is touched on only lightly in 2 Timothy.

There are more models of endurance Paul can present to Timothy. In 2:3–7, he simply mentions how the
soldier, the athlete, and the farmer must all undergo a
period of effort and self-denial if they are to receive the
reward of their labors. These examples are commonplace in Hellenistic moral exhortation, and are found
again in 1 Co 9:7,10,24. Here, Paul does not develop
the implications, but leaves it to Timothy to understand
the import of the examples (2:7).

The supreme example of suffering and reward for
both Paul and Timothy is, of course, Jesus. That Paul
is here reminding Timothy of that example is not clear
from the *JB* translation. A literal translation of 2:8
would read, "Remember Jesus Christ, raised from the

dead, sprung from the race of David." (A fuller version
of this elliptical summary of the Gospel can be found
in Rm 1:1–4). It is on account of his preaching of the
Good News about a crucified Messiah that Paul is in
chains. But he endures this suffering (2:10) for the
Gospel (2:9), for the sake of God's chosen ones
(2:10; cf. Ph 1:12–26). It is this kind of "sharing in
the suffering" for the Gospel that Paul wants Timothy
to endure with courage. They are both able to do this
because of the strength which comes from the Spirit of
Jesus (1:7,12), and because they know that, just as the
suffering of Jesus led to the new life of resurrection, so
also will their suffering with and for Jesus. To remind
Timothy of this surety, Paul quotes a traditional Christian hymn, introducing it with the peculiar rubric of the
Pastorals, "the word is faithful," or, as the *JB* renders
the Greek, "Here is a saying that you can rely on"
(2:11).

The hymn contains elements found elsewhere in
Paul (cf. 2 Co 7:3, Rm 6:8, 1 Co 4:8), but is struc-
tured in the antithetical style characteristic of some
sayings of Jesus and other judgment sayings in the New
Testament (cf. Mt 10:32–33, Mk 8:38, Lk 12:8–10, 1
Co 14:38). The first two statements are comforting: If
we die with Jesus, we will live with him; if we endure,
we will reign with him. Jesus is more than the model:
he is also the precursor. The third statement is frightening: "if we disown him, then he will disown us." But
the fourth statement, which climaxes the whole, creates
a stunning paradox. There is a correspondence between
our response to God and his response to us, yes. But it
is not a one-to-one correspondence. Even if we should
prove faithless, he remains faithful to his promise, to

himself. Here, Paul strikes again the genuine and distinctive note of his Gospel of God's grace (cf. Rm 3:3-4). Even human suffering and fidelity does not *win* favor from God. God's favor comes to us as a gift, and as an expression of his own faithfulness to humanity. And even when we turn away from him, his face is turned to us in love.

The faithfulness of God to those he has created, saved and called, provides the most secure hope for those who suffer because of their proclamation of the Gospel. This is Paul's most important reminder to Timothy.

STUDY QUESTION: Paul tells Timothy to remember the example of those who have suffered for the faith, and to take courage. What models do we have in our own lives of such fidelity in suffering?

2 Timothy 2:14–26
TIMOTHY'S OPPONENTS

14 Remind them of this; and tell them in the name of God that there is to be no wrangling about words: all that this ever achieves is the destruc-
15 tion of those who are listening. ·Do all you can to present yourself in front of God as a man who has come through his trials, and a man who has no cause to be ashamed of his life's work and has kept a straight course with the message of the
16 truth. ·Have nothing to do with pointless philosophical discussions—they only lead further and
17 further away from true religion. ·Talk of this kind corrodes like gangrene, as in the case of
18 Hymenaeus and Philetus, ·the men who have gone right away from the truth and claim that the resurrection has already taken place. Some people's faith cannot stand up to them.
19 However, God's solid foundation stone is still in position, and this is the inscription on it: "The Lord knows those who are his own" and "All who call on the name of the Lord must avoid sin."
20 Not all the dishes in a large house are made of gold and silver; some are made of wood or earthenware: some are kept for special occasions

²¹ and others are for ordinary purposes. ·Now, to avoid these faults that I am speaking about is the way for anyone to become a vessel for special occasions, fit for the Master himself to use, and kept ready for any good work.

²² Instead of giving in to your impulses like a young man, fasten your attention on holiness, faith, love and peace, in union with all those ²³ who call on the Lord with pure minds. ·Avoid these futile and silly speculations, understanding ²⁴ that they only give rise to quarrels; ·and a servant of the Lord is not to engage in quarrels, but has to be kind to everyone, a good teacher, and ²⁵ patient. ·He has to be gentle when he corrects people who dispute what he says, never forgetting that God may give them a change of mind so that ²⁶ they recognize the truth and ·come to their senses, once out of the trap where the devil caught them and kept them enslaved.

☩

Having presented himself as a model of endurance and sound teaching in the first part of the letter, Paul is now able to fill in that model by means of specific directives. As Paul has "reminded" Timothy, so Timothy in turn is to "remind" others of the ideal qualities of the Christian teacher, by exemplifying them in his own life (2:1). The focus in this section is unswervingly on Timothy's attitudes and actions. In order to illuminate the positive qualities which should be Timothy's ideal, Paul contrasts them at every step with the negative and harmful attitudes of the false teachers. Corresponding to every "do this" is an "avoid that."

The description of these false teachers is at once concrete and vague. Two of them (Hymenaeus and Philetus) are mentioned by name (2:17), and are said to be teaching that the resurrection (i.e. the resurrection of the believers) has already taken place. Their teaching may have resembled the position of some of Paul's Corinthian opponents, who seemed to hold that there was no future resurrection from the dead, since baptism had already brought about a resurrection life. But we cannot be sure. Nor can we state with certainty what conclusions these teachers may have been drawing from this position, since the rest of Paul's characterization deals not with specifics, but with the kind of broadside polemical condemnation frequently found in the disputes between opposing teachers in the Hellenistic world. Thus, we find generalized remarks on their morals, manners, and motivations, rather than on the specifics of their teaching. This is not a frontal attack on the false teachers, for they are certainly not the ones who will read this letter. Nor is such a polemic used by Paul to establish his own teaching by denigrating that of his opponents. Rather, this stylized form of polemic is here used as a foil to the positive image of the ideal teacher he is proposing to Timothy. This use of the polemic is well-attested in Hellenistic discourses which encourage young men to follow the life of virtue and philosophy; the philosophic ideal is portrayed negatively by the condemnation of those who bear the name of philosophers but shame it by their lives.

The fact that Paul is using a literary convention does not mean that these opponents were not real or troublesome. The passing remark later about Alexander the coppersmith in 4:14 indicates that real opposition to the Gospel is being experienced by Paul and Timothy alike. Indeed, this is the cause for Timothy's discouragement, that these opponents appear to be making such progress. But the stereotyped nature of the polemic makes it difficult for us to reconstruct exactly what ideas these men were proposing.

Depth psychology has furthered our understanding of humanity by teaching us that emotions are as real as ideas. It has, however, led to regression when interpreted to mean that only feelings are important, and that ideas are insignificant. The psychology of the ancients was sound in this, that it recognized how people act on their perceptions of the world. It was not, therefore, altogether beside the point to attack false ideas by condemning the immorality to which they led; for the truth in question was not abstract but existential, and existential error distorts life itself.

Paul diagnoses the "wrangling about words" (2:14), the "futile and silly discussions" (2:23), the "pointless philosophical discussions" (2:16) of the false teachers as a sickness of speech itself: it "corrodes like gangrene" (2:17). Such word-wrangling leads to quarrels (2:24) which are scarcely innocuous, since they lead in turn "to the destruction of those who are listening" (2:14). This is the final corruption caused by willful error, the loss of faith: "Some people's faith cannot stand up to them" (2:18).

Timothy is to avoid this kind of behavior in his own teaching (2:14,16,22,23,24). If he does so, he will be like that vessel in a household (filled with every sort of utensil) which is reserved by the master for his own use, because it is "ready for any good work" (2:21). In contrast to their sick speech, Timothy will keep "a straight course with the message of the truth" (2:15). In contrast to their revolutionary impulses (2:22, a plausible rendering of the Greek), Timothy will devote himself to those qualities of holiness, faith, love and peace which he found exemplified in his model, Paul (1:13). In contrast to their quarrelsomeness, he will be "kind to everyone, a good teacher, and patient" (2:24).

Given the harshness of these opponents, it is somewhat surprising to find the attitude Paul recommends Timothy to adopt toward them. He is to avoid their methods, to be sure, but he is not told to avoid them. Nor is he to deal harshly or in a condemnatory manner toward them. Rather, he is to be "gentle when he corrects people who dispute his teaching," with the hope that they too can come to see the truth and be freed from their enslavement to error (2:25–26). This irenic attitude and pastoral care for the opponents is distinctive of 2 Timothy. In the other Pastorals, Paul's attitude hardens somewhat. But here, he does not see them simply as "vessels fit for destruction" (cf. Rm 9:22) so much as wanderers from the truth who, by the good and gentle example of the true teacher, might themselves become "special vessels" in the household of the Lord (cf. 2:20–21).

STUDY QUESTION: Would Paul agree with the attitude toward truth and error which is expressed in the statement, "It doesn't matter what you believe so long as your heart is in the right place"?

2 Timothy 3:1–17
TIMOTHY'S TRIBULATIONS

3 1 You may be quite sure that in the last days there are going to be some difficult times.
2 People will be self-centered and grasping; boastful, arrogant and rude; disobedient to their
3 parents, ungrateful, irreligious; ·heartless and unappeasable; they will be slanderers, profligates, savages and enemies of everything that is good;
4 they will be treacherous and reckless and demented by pride, preferring their own pleasure
5 to God. ·They will keep up the outward appearance of religion but will have rejected the inner power of it. Have nothing to do with people like that.
6 Of the same kind, too, are those men who insinuate themselves into families in order to get influence over silly women who are obsessed with their sins and follow one craze after another
7 in the attempt to educate themselves, but can
8 never come to knowledge of the truth. ·Men like this defy the truth just as Jannes and Jambres defied Moses: their minds are corrupt and their
9 faith spurious. ·But they will not be able to go on

any longer: their foolishness, like that of the other two, must become obvious to everybody.

10 You know, though, what I have taught, how I have lived, what I have aimed at; you know my faith, my patience and my love; my constancy 11 and the persecutions and hardships that came to me in places like Antioch, Iconium and Lystra—all the persecutions I have endured; and the Lord 12 has rescued me from every one of them. ·You are well aware, then, that anybody who tries to live in devotion to Christ is certain to be attacked; 13 while these wicked impostors will go from bad to worse, deceiving others and deceived themselves.

14 You must keep to what you have been taught and know to be true; remember who your teach- 15 ers were, ·and how, ever since you were a child, you have known the holy scriptures—from these you can learn the wisdom that leads to salvation 16 through faith in Christ Jesus. ·All scripture is inspired by God and can profitably be used for teaching, for refuting error, for guiding people's 17 lives and teaching them to be holy. ·This is how the man who is dedicated to God becomes fully equipped and ready for any good work.

✠

The heart of this passage lies in verses 13–14: "these wicked impostors will go from bad to worse, deceiving others and deceived themselves. . . . You must keep to what you have been taught and know to be true." Paul continues his presentation of the teaching ideal by means of contrast to the opponents. Timothy is to recognize in their manner both the characteristics of the opponents of the end-time (3:1–5), and

the style of those impostors who have always opposed
God's emissaries, as the magicians of Pharaoh's court
opposed Moses (3:8).

That the elect were to experience tribulation and opposition before the triumphant return of the Lord was
a commonplace of early Christian understanding. And
a dominant feature of the tribulation was the coming of
false teachers who "will arise and lead many astray"
(Mt 24:11, Mk 13:22, Lk 21:8, Ac 20:29–30, 2 Th
2:3–12, 1 Jn 4:1, Rv 13:13). The real danger of these
false teachers lay in their plausibility. They proclaimed
the Christ, but in such fashion that the truth of Christ
was distorted. Precisely the power they wielded as religious figures was dangerous, because it was deceptive.
They had "the outward appearance of religion but will
have rejected the inner power of it" (3:5). In the long
vice-list of 3:1–5, which picks up several of the terms
from the vice-list of Rm 1:30–31, Paul piles up all the
extravagant, self-centered and antisocial vices he can
think of, to condemn these impostors.

The word "impostor" (Greek: *goēs*) is itself in-
teresting, since it is a word which in the Hellenistic culture pointed at once to splashy display of power and
lack of inner spiritual conviction. Thus, Jannes and
Jambres, the magicians of Pharaoh's court (their
names are not found in Ex 7:11,22 but are supplied
frequently in Jewish tradition) were able to duplicate
the feats of Moses and Aaron, but were not able to
resist the overwhelming power of God which liberated
Israel from Egypt. *That* was real power, the power of
the truth. Paul reminds Timothy of this to encourage
him: "They will not be able to go on any longer; their

foolishness, like that of the other two, must become
obvious to everybody" (3:9).

But the imminent collapse of the opponents does not
now seem so obvious. In fact, they are enjoying great
success, and are disrupting households by influencing
those least able to resist their spiritual charms: unedu-
cated and emotionally troubled women (3:6-8). The
dilemma of powerless and undereducated women in
Paul's day was no less serious and tragic than today.
Despite the condescension of his language ("silly
women"), Paul is not making a statement about the in-
nate neuroticism or uneducability of women. Remember that Timothy was educated in the faith by
women. Paul is simply stating the facts of his situation:
that those who by status and learning were least able to
repel hucksterism were being taken in by counterfeit
claims.

The success of these false teachers is a genuine
source of suffering to Paul's delegate. Therefore, when
Paul again presents himself to Timothy as a model
(3:10-11), he includes not only the qualities he should
imitate, but especially reminds him of all the tribulations from which the Lord delivered him (3:11). He
states as axiomatic that anyone who tries to live in devotion to Christ will suffer (cf. also Ac 14:22), and
implies that as the Lord delivered him from all these
trials, so will Timothy be delivered.

In contrast to the specious "progress" of the false
teachers, which is really a progression from bad to
worse (3:13), Timothy is to root himself ever more
deeply in the tradition he has received. He is to imitate
the model he has in Paul (3:10-11), and the faith of
those holy women who were his teachers in the faith

(3:14; cf. 1:5). Above all, he is to be a student of the
Scriptures, for "from these you can learn the wisdom
that leads to salvation through faith in Jesus Christ"
(3:15). The important thing about Paul's characterization of the Scriptures is not simply that he asserts
their divine inspiration. The conviction that the Scriptures were God's inspired word was fundamental to the
Christian faith and not remarkable. What is significant
here is Paul's insistence that the Christian teacher must
be steeped in this divine word, shaped him or herself
by its truth. Only then can the teacher employ its message, not as a bludgeon for the beating of heretics, but
as the delicate instrument of instruction; which, in "refuting error" has nothing to do with the disputa-
tiousness of the false teachers, and everything to do
with "guiding people's lives" and "teaching them to be
holy" (3:16).

STUDY QUESTION: Is there something about the Gospel
                 message itself which should shape
                 the qualities of gentleness, patience
                 and endurance in the Christian
                 teacher?

2 Timothy 4:1–22
THE LABOR AND ITS REWARD

¹ 4 Before God and before Christ Jesus who is to be judge of the living and the dead, I put this duty to you, in the name of his Appearing ² and of his kingdom: ·proclaim the message and, welcome or unwelcome, insist on it. Refute falsehood, correct error, call to obedience—but do all with patience and with the intention of teaching. ³ The time is sure to come when, far from being content with sound teaching, people will be avid for the latest novelty and collect themselves a whole series of teachers according to their own ⁴ tastes; ·and then, instead of listening to the truth, ⁵ they will turn to myths. ·Be careful always to choose the right course; be brave under trials; make the preaching of the Good News your life's work, in thoroughgoing service.

⁶ As for me, my life is already being poured away as a libation, and the time has come for me ⁷ to be gone. ·I have fought the good fight to the end: I have run the race to the finish; I have kept ⁸ the faith; ·all there is to come now is the crown of righteousness reserved for me, which the Lord,

the righteous judge, will give to me on that Day; and not only to me but to all those who have longed for his Appearing.

9 Do your best to come and see me as soon as
10 you can. ·As it is, Demas has deserted me for love of this life and gone to Thessalonika, Crescens
11 has gone to Galatia and Titus to Dalmatia; ·only Luke is with me. Get Mark to come and bring him with you; I find him a useful helper in
12 my work. ·I have sent Tychicus to Ephesus.
13 When you come, bring the cloak I left with Carpus in Troas, and the scrolls, especially the
14 parchment ones. ·Alexander the coppersmith has done me a lot of harm: the Lord will repay him
15 for what he has done. ·Be on your guard against him yourself, because he has been bitterly contesting everything that we say.

16 The first time I had to present my defense, there was not a single witness to support me. Every one of them deserted me—may they not be
17 held accountable for it. ·But the Lord stood by me and gave me power, so that through me the whole message might be proclaimed for all the pagans to hear; and so I was rescued from the
18 lion's mouth. ·The Lord will rescue me from all evil attempts on me, and bring me safely to his heavenly kingdom. To him be glory for ever and ever. Amen.

19 Greetings to Prisca and Aquila, and the family
20 of Onesiphorus. ·Erastus remained at Corinth,
21 and I left Trophimus ill at Miletus. ·Do your best to come before the winter.

Greetings to you from Eubulus, Pudens, Linus, Claudia and all the brothers.

22 The Lord be with your spirit. Grace be with you.

✠

Paul concludes his exhortation of Timothy with a solemn and urgent charge to stand fast and persevere in his work as a teacher and proclaimer of the Good News (4:1–8). The task is difficult for Timothy now, and it will grow more arduous still, as the time before the coming of the Lord draws nearer. The false teachers will find more and more people willing to abandon the healthy teaching of the Gospel (4:3) in favor of the seductive myths which cater to their own fancy (4:4). This is not an optimistic view of the future. Paul senses that his own abandonment by his helpers (4:10, 1:15) is part of a wider turning away from the truth of the Gospel. And as he faces his own death, he is the more concerned to encourage his associate to continue the "good fight to the end" (4:7).

It is striking that in the face of this rejection, Paul does not tell Timothy to grow rigid or harsh, but continues to emphasize those qualities of gentleness and patience which should always mark the Christian teacher, in bad times as well as good. The hope shared by Paul and Timothy is not based in their human success. It is, rather, that the "judge of the living and the dead" will, in the establishment of His kingdom (4:1), reward them with the "crown of righteousness" reserved for those who have truly loved the Lord and done his service (cf. Rm 8:28, 1 Co 2:9, Ph 3:14, 1 P 5:4, Jm 1:12, Rv 2:10). Paul had proposed to Timothy in 2:5 the example of the athlete who, if he

competes according to the rules, will win the crown.
The pertinence of that example now becomes clear, as
Paul speaks of himself as just such an athlete, "I have
run the race to the finish, I have kept the faith" (4:7;
cf. also Ph 2:16, 3:14). He now confidently awaits
the crown reserved for him and for "all those who have
longed for his Appearing" (4:8), among whom,
clearly, he hopes Timothy will continue to be counted.

It is difficult to avoid the impression that it is not
only Timothy's discouragement with which Paul must
contend, but his own as well. This final charge to Timothy is filled with pathos. Whether Paul died shortly
after this letter or not, he was certainly expecting to.
The Apostle who formerly had given thanks to God,
who "makes us, in Christ, partners of his triumph, and
through us is spreading the knowledge of himself" (2
Co 2:14), is now imprisoned, abandoned, and fearful
lest the message of Christ be distorted or lost. But even
in these circumstances, he continues, so far as he is
able, to direct the work of the mission (4:11-15). And
even in these circumstances, he is able to transcend his
own discouragement and reach out in comfort and exhortation to his troubled associate. Paul's confidence
was rooted, ultimately, not in himself, but in the Lord,
who "stood by me and gave me power" and who, in
the end, would "bring me safely to his heavenly kingdom" (4:17-18). Paul has indeed shown, by this letter, that "they cannot chain up God's news" (2:9),
that he himself had fought the good fight to the end
and kept the faith (4:7) in a fashion worthy of imitation by Timothy and "anybody who tries to live in devotion to Christ" (3:12).

STUDY QUESTION: Is the significance of 2 Timothy restricted to those whose express ministry is that of teaching and preaching, or does it extend to all in the Church?

1 Timothy
"How to Behave in God's Family"

The setting and shape of 1 Timothy have differences from 2 Timothy. Paul is not in prison, but is actively moving about in his ministry. He has left for Macedonia, and instructed Timothy to remain in Ephesus to set matters straight there, till he returns (1:3, 3:14). Until he comes, he wishes Timothy to preach, teach, and present himself as a model to that community (4:12–13). To equip him for this task, Paul writes instructions concerning the proper attitude Timothy should have in his teaching, and specific instructions concerning various groups within the community. He wants Timothy to have guidelines for "how people ought to behave in God's family—that is, in the Church of the living God" (3:15).

The personal reminders to Timothy of his teaching task resemble, when taken together, the form of personal paraenetic letter we have seen in 2 Timothy (cf. the introduction to the Pastorals). But 1 Timothy lacks that letter's tight literary coherence. The directives concerning presiding elders, deacons and widows (3:1–13, 5:1–21), slaves (6:1–2), the rich (6:17–19) and the behavior of men and women in worship (2:1–15) occur in blocks separate from the personal exhortations to Timothy (1:3–20, 3:14–4:16, 6:2–16, 6:20–21).

This letter has a little more detailed information about the false teachers. We are told that they wish to be teachers of the law (1:7), claim to have special knowledge (6:20), have an ascetic tendency, which manifests itself in the prohibition of marriage and certain foods (4:3), and a rigorous physical regimen (4:8). In contrast to 2 Timothy, Paul here corrects some of their misunderstandings (1:8–11, 4:1–5, 6:6–8). Generally, however, he uses the same general polemic as in 2 Timothy as a foil for the positive ideal of the Christian teacher he encourages his associate to pursue. The main focus of this small commentary will be on those materials not shared with 2 Timothy, the instructions on church order.

For many commentators, these instructions are the biggest barrier to recognizing this letter as genuinely Pauline. They point out that this attention to organizational detail is lacking in his other letters, and may conflict with the picture of a charismatic church such as we find portrayed in 1 Corinthians. But the organizational structure found here appears as primitive as that suggested by the greeting of Philippians 1:1, and is consistent with the sort of synagogal structure of diaspora Judaism, to which the Church undoubtedly looked for its first arrangement. More pertinently, while discussion of the qualifications of elders, and so forth, would hardly be appropriate in letters written to whole communities, it is just the sort of matter we would expect to find discussed in a letter written to a delegate whose role it was to stabilize a church in the absence of the apostle. The disjointed presentation of these matters, here, argues for their *ad hoc* nature, and suggests that we should see in 1 Timothy not a full blown "Church Order," but only the first step in the development of such documents within the Church.

1 Timothy 1:1–20
THE TEACHING OF LAW AND THE GOSPEL OF GRACE

1 From Paul, apostle of Christ Jesus appointed by the command of God our savior and of
2 Christ Jesus our hope, ·to Timothy, true child of mine in the faith; wishing you grace, mercy and peace from God the Father and from Christ Jesus our Lord.

3 As I asked you when I was leaving for Macedonia, please stay at Ephesus, to insist that certain people stop teaching strange doctrines
4 and taking notice of myths and endless genealogies; these things are only likely to raise irrelevant doubts instead of furthering the designs of
5 God which are revealed in faith. ·The only purpose of this instruction is that there should be love, coming out of a pure heart, a clear con-
6 science and a sincere faith. ·There are some people who have gone off the straight course and
7 taken a road that leads to empty speculation; ·they claim to be doctors of the Law but they understand neither the arguments they are using nor the opinions they are upholding.

8 We know, of course, that the Law is good, but

⁹ only provided it is treated like any law, ·in the understanding that laws are not framed for people who are good. On the contrary, they are for criminals and revolutionaries, for the irreligious and the wicked, for the sacrilegious and the irreverent; they are for people who kill their fathers ¹⁰ or mothers and for murderers, ·for those who are immoral with women or with boys or with men, for liars and for perjurers—and for everything else that is contrary to the sound teaching ¹¹ that goes with the Good News of the glory of the blessed God, the gospel that was entrusted to me.

¹² I thank Christ Jesus our Lord, who has given me strength, and who judged me faithful enough ¹³ to call me into his service ·even though I used to be a blasphemer and did all I could to injure and discredit the faith. Mercy, however, was shown me, because until I became a believer I ¹⁴ had been acting in ignorance; ·and the grace of our Lord filled me with faith and with the love ¹⁵ that is in Christ Jesus. ·Here is a saying that you can rely on and nobody should doubt: that Christ Jesus came into the world to save sinners. I my-¹⁶ self am the greatest of them; ·and if mercy has been shown to me, it is because Jesus Christ meant to make me the greatest evidence of his inexhaustible patience for all the other people who would later have to trust in him to come to ¹⁷ eternal life. ·To the eternal King, the undying, invisible and only God, be honor and glory for ever and ever. Amen.

¹⁸ Timothy, my son, these are the instructions that I am giving you: I ask you to remember the words once spoken over you by the prophets, and taking them to heart to fight like a good ¹⁹ soldier ·with faith and a good conscience for your weapons. Some people have put conscience aside ²⁰ and wrecked their faith in consequence. ·I mean men like Hymenaeus and Alexander, whom I

have handed over to Satan to teach them not to
be blasphemous.

✠

There is no opening thanksgiving here. Paul turns at
once to the reasons he left Timothy in Ephesus. Paul
wants him to order "certain people" to stop teaching
strange doctrines. The bizarre "myths and genealogies"
(1:4) which are the doctrinal baggage of these would-
be teachers of the Law (1:7) are not just foolish
(1:6); they are dangerous. The healthy teaching of the
Gospel (1:10) reveals to people the "designs of God
in faith" (1:4; cf. Col 1:25), and leads them to love, a
good conscience, and genuine faith (1:5). The false
teachers are apparently trying to reestablish the Law of
Moses as the basis of Christian life, and themselves as
arbiters of Christian behavior. But they have "put conscience aside and wrecked their faith in consequence"
(1:19), and, allowing the Law to be their standard,
have effectively denied the significance of God's grace
in Jesus Christ (cf. Ga 3:1–5, 4:1–7, 5:2–6, Col
2:20–23). Paul sees this as the most wrongheaded sort
of enterprise: "They understand neither the arguments
they are using nor the opinions they are upholding"
(1:7). These teachers do not build up faith, but merely
raise "irrelevant doubts" (1:4).

Paul would never deny the Law's status as "holy and
just and good" (Rm 7:12,16; cf. 1:8), since it came
from God, and revealed to humans their rebellion
against the Father. But he denies vigorously and every-

where the power of the Law to save. And for one who
has been made "righteous" (the *JB* has "people who
are good" for this Pauline expression in 1:9) by the
grace of God revealed by the Gospel, the Law strictly
does not apply (1:9). Its role is the manifesting of
wickedness, the many varieties of which Paul enumer-
ates in the vice-list of 1:9–10; it cannot save.

The terminology in this discussion is somewhat unu-
sual: Paul ordinarily speaks of "strong" and "weak"
consciences, for example, rather than "good" or
"bad"; but the debate is a familiar one. Paul constantly
defended the primacy of the Gospel against the preten-
sions of the Law.

Although it is typical of Paul to attach an account of
his own call to the mention of the Gospel (1:12–17),
it is here in the form of a thanksgiving. We should not
miss the significance of this following the statements
about the Law, for Paul presents himself here as the
model of one saved by grace. Before his conversion, he
was the most devout observer of the Law (Ga 1:14, Ph
3:6). If salvation could have come through such observance, it would have come to him. But since he
resisted the call to believe in God's grace revealed
through Jesus, by standing on his own righteousness,
he was a blasphemer and persecutor of the Church
(1:13). He acted in "ignorance" (1:13), as did those
Jews, who "being ignorant of the righteousness that
comes from God, and seeking to establish their own,
did not submit to God's righteousness" (Rm 10:3). In
this rebellion, precisely on the basis of observing the
Law, was Paul shown to be a sinner.

But the grace of God overcame even his resistance,
establishing him in faith and in apostleship. Paul, then,

can affirm the "reliability" of this traditional statement, "Christ Jesus came into the world to save sinners," for, "I myself am the greatest of them" (1:15). He stands, therefore, as an example to all those who live by faith and not by the Law, and even more, as an example of God's "inexhaustible patience" (1:16). Paul concludes this thanksgiving with a solemn doxology (1:17), and briskly returns to his exhortation of Timothy.

Again, Timothy's call to "fight like a good soldier" in his ministry is based on the recollection of his appointment (cf. 2 Tm 1:6), which Paul here says was accompanied by prophetic utterances (cf. Ac 13:1-3), and is contrasted to the behavior of the false teachers (1:19-20). Two of them, Hymenaeus (2 Tm 2:17) and Alexander (2 Tm 4:14?), Paul has "handed over to Satan to teach them not to be blasphemous" (1:20). We don't know quite what this means, though it is probably a form of temporary exclusion from the community for the purpose of discipline, similar to that mentioned in 1 Co 5:5.

STUDY QUESTIONS: What effect did Paul's conversion experience have on his perception of the Christian Mystery? What effect has your personal experience of the Lord had on your perception of the faith?

1 Timothy 2:1–15
WOMEN AND MEN IN WORSHIP

[1] 2 My advice is that, first of all, there should be
prayers offered for everyone—petitions, inter-
[2] cessions and thanksgiving—·and especially for
kings and others in authority, so that we may be
able to live religious and reverent lives in peace
[3] and quiet. ·To do this is right, and will please
[4] God our Savior: ·he wants everyone to be saved
[5] and reach full knowledge of the truth. ·For there
is only one God, and there is only one mediator
between God and mankind, himself a man, Christ
[6] Jesus, ·who sacrificed himself as a ransom for
them all. He is the evidence of this, sent at the
[7] appointed time, and ·I have been named a herald
and apostle of it and—I am telling the truth and
no lie—a teacher of the faith and the truth to the
pagans.
[8]   In every place, then, I want the men to lift their
hands up reverently in prayer, with no anger or
argument.
[9]   Similarly, I direct that women are to wear
suitable clothes and to be dressed quietly and
modestly, without braided hair or gold and jew-

¹⁰ elry or expensive clothes; their adornment is ·to
do the sort of good works that are proper for
¹¹ women who profess to be religious. ·During in-
struction, a woman should be quiet and respect-
¹² ful. ·I am not giving permission for a woman to
teach or to tell a man what to do. A woman ought
¹³ not to speak, ·because Adam was formed first and
¹⁴ Eve afterward, ·and it was not Adam who was
led astray but the woman who was led astray and
¹⁵ fell into sin. ·Nevertheless, she will be saved by
childbearing, provided she lives a modest life and
is constant in faith and love and holiness.

✠

Paul's first instructions on "how people ought to behave in the family of God" (cf. 3:15) concern good
order in worship. What the *JB* translates as "family" is,
literally, "household," and these instructions stress the
same proper observance of roles and submission, as did
the ethics of the Hellenistic household (cf. commentary
on Col 3:18–4:1). The roles of men and women in
worship correspond to what we know of the customs of
the synagogue: men led the prayers (2:8), read and
preached; women kept silence in the public assembly
(2:11–12). Although women played an important role
in Jewish domestic liturgies, it was considered shameful
in that culture for women to take a dominant role in
any public affair. Equally shameful was the use of a
worship service as an occasion for displaying fine
clothing and jewels (2:9; cf. 1 P 3:1–6). What the culture expected of virtuous women, Paul demanded of

Christian wives: the silent testimony of modesty, submission, and works of charity (2:10).

These instructions on the place of women in worship resemble those in 1 Co 11:3–6 and 14:33–35. But there, Paul showed signs of struggling with the tension between the demands of tradition (11:2, 14:34) and the impulses of the Spirit, which were leading women to prophesy in the assembly (11:5). The vehemence of his stand on tradition, there and here, suggests that the Spirit was bursting the bounds even of Paul's ability to perceive.

In an age when women were only grudgingly granted the status of humanity by some, Paul's statements regarding the equality of men and women in Christ were a significant advance; as a man conditioned by the societal norms of his age, he was not able to advance further. So strong was the tradition, that Paul could conclude that the proper role of women consisted simply in childbearing (2:15). Attempts to read this verse in a more enlightened fashion, as "she will be saved through the birth of the child" (i.e. the Messiah), or, "she will be brought safely through childbirth," do not work, and miss the point that Paul is just stating what was axiomatic for his time. Indeed, Paul sharpens this by a reading of the Genesis story of the fall which lacks his usual careful qualifications (contrast 1 Co 11:8–12, 2 Co 11:3, Rm 5:12).

But more than tradition may be at work here. It appears from 5:13, 2 Tm 3:6, and Tt 1:11, that the false teachers are making their greatest inroads precisely among women, with the result that whole families are being disrupted (Tt 1:11). Paul's emphasis on the subordinate role of women may here owe something to his

wanting to strengthen the community's resistance to
these charlatans.

The picture of community worship here is neither as
full nor colorful as that in 1 Co 11,12–14. There is
only the barest summary of what would take place in a
service: petitions, intercessions and thanksgivings
(2:1). It is not remarkable that political rulers are to
be prayed for (2:2), but Paul attaches to this commonplace recommendation one of his most important
and far-reaching statements of God's salvific will: "he
wants everyone to be saved and reach full knowledge
of the truth" (2:4). This is a proposition whose full
implications have yet to be assimilated by Christians.
The basis of this breathtaking assertion is simply the
nature of God and his gift. God is not the peculiar possession of either Jews or Christians. He is the one God
of all humanity (cf. Rm 3:29–30), whose gift of life
witnessed by the saving death of the one mediator, the
man Jesus Christ (2:5), has the most profound conse-
quences for all humanity.

STUDY QUESTION: If God wills all people to be saved,
and his will is effective, what
difference does it make if one is or
is not a Christian?

1 Timothy 3:1-16
THE QUALITIES OF COMMUNITY LEADERS

¹ 3 Here is a saying that you can rely on: To want to be a presiding elder is to want to do a noble ² work. ·That is why the president must have an impeccable character. He must not have been married more than once, and he must be temperate, discreet and courteous, hospitable and a good ³ teacher; ·not a heavy drinker, not hot-tempered, but kind and peaceable. He must not be a lover of ⁴ money. ·He must be a man who manages his own family well and brings his children up to obey him ⁵ and be well-behaved: ·how can any man who does not understand how to manage his own family ⁶ have responsibility for the church of God? ·He should not be a new convert, in case pride might turn his head and then he might be condemned as ⁷ the devil was condemned. ·It is also necessary that people outside the Church should speak well of him, so that he never gets a bad reputation and falls into the devil's trap.

⁸ In the same way, deacons must be respectable men whose word can be trusted, moderate in the amount of wine they drink and with no squalid

⁹ greed for money. ·They must be conscientious
¹⁰ believers in the mystery of the faith. ·They are
to be examined first, and only admitted to serve
¹¹ as deacons if there is nothing against them. ·In
the same way, the women must be respectable,
¹² not gossips but sober and quite reliable. ·Dea-
cons must not have been married more than
once, and must be men who manage their chil-
¹³ dren and families well. ·Those of them who carry
out their duties well as deacons will earn a high
standing for themselves and be rewarded with
great assurance in their work for the faith in
Christ Jesus.

¹⁴   At the moment of writing to you, I am hoping
¹⁵ that I may be with you soon; ·but in case I
should be delayed, I wanted you to know how
people ought to behave in God's family—that is,
in the Church of the living God, which upholds
¹⁶ the truth and keeps it safe. ·Without any doubt,
the mystery of our religion is very deep indeed:

> He was made visible in the flesh,
> attested by the Spirit,
> seen by angels,
> proclaimed to the pagans,
> believed in by the world,
> taken up in glory.

✠

Paul next turns his attention to the qualifications
Timothy should look for in those exercising ministries
of supervision and service within the Church. Little is
said here about the duties of these ministers, for Paul is
not so much drawing up a new job description, as reminding Timothy of the moral character needed by

such leaders if the Church is to enjoy a good reputation.

Our natural curiosity about the authority structure of the community is consequently frustrated. It is not clear, for example, whether the position of the "bishop" (which the *JB* judiciously translates as "presiding elder") is the same as that of "elder." One of the qualities recommended for the "presiding elder" is aptness in teaching; in 5:17, Paul says that "elders in charge" should be given double consideration when they preach and teach. Paul's other letters do not help. Although he mentions bishops and deacons in Ph 1:1, he does not say what they do, and he nowhere speaks of elders, although they appear elsewhere in the New Testament as leaders of communities (cf. Ac 11:30, 14:23, 15:2–4, 20:17,28—elders and bishops appearing interchangeable—Jm 5:14, 1 P 5:1). Apart from the function of teaching (which seems to be an additional or optional task), the kinds of qualities listed seem to suggest administrative functions at different levels. We know that the Jewish synagogue had a board of elders (cf. 4:14—"body of elders") which saw to good order and handled finances, and it is not unreasonable to suggest that the first Christian communities adopted this authority structure. But certainty is not possible.

We should certainly avoid anachronism when reading these passages. There is no hint here of the "monarchical episcopate" found in the letters of Ignatius of Antioch (ca. A.D. 115), or the concentration of priestly, prophetic and pastoral roles in the office of the bishop, such as we find in later Church history.

Paul does speak elsewhere of the ministries of

"teaching, helping, administering" (1 Co 12:28); "serving, teaching, helping" (Rm 12:7-8); "pastoring, teaching" (Ep 4:11), among the charismatic gifts of the community. That spirit-filled connection is not drawn explicitly here, although these ministers are appointed by the "laying on of hands" (5:22), and in Timothy's case, that appointment was connected with prophecy and the gift of the Spirit (1 Tm 1:18, 4:14, 2 Tm 1:6). Because the point of the passage is not the description of church order but the inculcation of virtue, the understandable desire of historians to draw conclusions from it concerning the development of authority within the early Church is hazardous. It seems equally unlikely that the Pastorals reflect a church completely without charism and 1 Corinthians a church completely without structure.

The pervasive influence of the "household" model continues in this passage. The Church is described as the "household of God" (*JB:* "God's family"), which, in the face of opposition from false teachers must manifest "the living God" by "upholding the truth and keeping it safe" (3:15). The Greek underlying the *JB* picks up the architectural imagery of the house: the Church is to be the "pillar and bulwark of the truth" (3:15). The image of the Church as a building, which in Ep 2:20-22 was organic and dynamic, has here taken on a more defensive tone. Confronted with distortion of its message, the Church now must clearly and unequivocally manifest the "health" of its teaching. And this should nowhere be clearer than in the lives of her leaders.

The list of virtues prescribed for the bishops, deacons (and perhaps deaconesses, cf. 3:11) is not an ex-

haustive inventory of the Christian life, but suggests the
kinds of virtues necessary to people exercising authority. They are summed up in the model of the good father in a Hellenistic household: "How can any man
who does not understand how to manage his own family have responsibility for the church of God?"
(3:5,12). Maturity in the faith, marital fidelity, freedom from greed, and trustworthiness may not appear
particularly heroic to those whose notions of the heroic
come from romances rather than life. But they are expressions of a more than "bourgeois piety" when lived
by those whose behavior is the standard by which outsiders judge the character of the community as a whole.

Paul concludes this series of directives by reminding
Timothy of the "mystery of our religion" (3:16). He
does this by quoting what appears to be a portion of a
traditional hymn about the appearance and glorifica-
tion of Christ (cf. commentary on Col 1:15–20). The
style of the hymn recalls 1 P 1:20, 3:18–22, which
may also have been dependent on a traditional hymn.
Terms such as "flesh" and "Spirit" appear to reflect
normal Pauline usage, but the combinations are not
quite what we would expect. So the Greek underlying
"attested by the Spirit" is "was justified by (or in) the
Spirit." This comes closest, in the Pauline writings, to
the summary of the Gospel in Rm 1:3–4, which is also
traditional. It is because Christ has entered into the
realm of God's own life, has been "taken up in glory"
that the Gospel which has been "proclaimed to the pagans" has been "believed in by the world." The elements of "manifestation" and "proclaiming" seem to
provide the basis for the citation of the hymn here. The

Church is to proclaim by its word and manifest in its life the power of God's work in Jesus to the world.

STUDY QUESTION: Why is there no discussion of "priests" in Paul's discussion of Christian ministers?

1 Timothy 4:1–16
HEALTHY TEACHING LEADS TO FREEDOM

1 4 The Spirit has explicitly said that during the last times there will be some who will desert the faith and choose to listen to deceitful spirits
2 and doctrines that come from the devils; ·and the cause of this is the lies told by hypocrites whose consciences are branded as though with a
3 red-hot iron: ·they will say marriage is forbidden, and lay down rules about abstaining from foods which God created to be accepted with thanksgiving by all who believe and who know
4 the truth. ·Everything God has created is good, and no food is to be rejected, provided grace is
5 said for it: ·the word of God and the prayer
6 make it holy. ·If you put all this to the brothers, you will be a good servant of Christ Jesus and show that you have really digested the teaching of the faith and the good doctrine which you
7 have always followed. ·Have nothing to do with godless myths and old wives' tales. Train your-
8 self spiritually. ·"Physical exercises are useful enough, but the usefulness of spirituality is unlimited, since it holds out the reward of life here and now and of the future life as well";

⁹ that is a saying that you can rely on and nobody
¹⁰ should doubt it. ·I mean that the point of all our
toiling and battling is that we have put our trust
in the living God and he is the savior of the
whole human race but particularly of all believ-
¹¹ ers. ·This is what you are to enforce in your
teaching.
¹² Do not let people disregard you because you
are young, but be an example to all the believers in the way you speak and behave, and in
¹³ your love, your faith and your purity. ·Make use
of the time until I arrive by reading to the peo-
¹⁴ ple, preaching and teaching. ·You have in you a
spiritual gift which was given to you when the
prophets spoke and the body of elders laid their
¹⁵ hands on you; do not let it lie unused. ·Think
hard about all this, and put it into practice, and
everyone will be able to see how you are advanc-
¹⁶ ing. ·Take great care about what you do and
what you teach; always do this, and in this way
you will save both yourself and those who listen
to you.

✠

Paul returns now to his personal exhortation of Timothy, fashioning for him, by way of contrast to the opponents, a picture of the ideal teacher. We saw in 2 Tm
1:13 how Paul presented himself as model teacher
to Timothy. Here also, if Timothy teaches sound doctrine as he learned it from Paul (4:6), he will be a
"good servant of Christ Jesus." But Paul wants Timothy to do more than follow his example: he wants
him to become himself a model to all the believers, not
only in what he teaches, but in all his actions (4:12).

All of Timothy's "reading, preaching and teaching" (4:13) will be useless unless he makes effective in his life the spiritual gift which was given to him (4:14). But when the words of the preacher emerge from a life in which the Spirit's power is active, then the words of a human being can become that Word which saves both the one speaking and those who listen (4:16).

Paul wants Timothy to avoid the "godless myths and old wives' tales" of the false teachers (4:7), whose consciences are as numb as if they had been cauterized by a branding iron, and whose piety and asceticism based on observance of the Law come from hypocrisy (4:2). Strong words, probably made more so because some of the things being taught by the opponents could represent exaggerations or misunderstandings of Paul's own distinctive teaching. We can see already in 1 Corinthians how Paul's preaching could be taken to extremes he later felt needed correction. And if these teachers say that Christians are not permitted to marry (4:3), they could find some support for that position in Paul's clear preference for virginity expressed in 1 Co 7:1–7. It is more probable, however, that these opponents were not "radical Paulinists" but Jewish-Christians who, in their desire to impose the Law on others, imposed as well the kind of rigorous asceticism we have seen promulgated by the opponents in Colossae (cf. commentary on Col 2:6 – 3:4). We find here the litany of "do not touch, do not handle, do not taste" (cf. Col 2:21). Paul's reaction is vigorous. How can there be such limits placed on the experience of the world, when the world and all that is in it come from the creative hand of God? "Everything God has created is good, and no food is to be rejected" (4:4).

This is a statement of the freedom of Christians as
ringing as that in Ga 5:1: "For Freedom Christ has
freed you." The blessing of food, that is, the thanksgiving said by believers before eating, is not an exor-
cism of what is wicked, but a simple recognition of
God's gift. The word of God and prayer (4:5) do not
make food holy by incantation, but by the acknowl-
edgment that all which comes from God deserves blessing and praise.

Timothy is also to reject that negative attitude toward the body which is expressed by an excessive physical asceticism (4:8). Such flogging of the body not
only despises the goodness of God's creation, but turns
into a spiritual narcissism (cf. Col 2:23). It is worth-
less for service toward others (4:8), for it is just another form of self-preoccupation. The "spiritual training" Paul calls Timothy to (4:8) is precisely that
"toiling and battling" for the Gospel which has marked
Paul's own life (cf. 1 Co 9:25, 15:10, Ga 4:11, Ph
2:16, 1 Th 5:12, Col 1:29, 4:12–13), and which is an
expression of "trust in the living God" that salvation
comes not from our own efforts, but from him who "is
the savior of the whole human race but particularly of
all believers" (4:10).

STUDY QUESTION: How can one account for the con-
tinued popularity of physical asceticism as a sign of virtue, in the
face of the New Testament's negative attitude toward it?

1 Timothy 5:1–16
THE CARE OF WIDOWS

1 5 Do not speak harshly to a man older than
yourself, but advise him as you would your
own father; treat the younger men as brothers
2 and older women as you would your mother.
Always treat young women with propriety, as if
they were sisters.

3 Be considerate to widows; I mean those who
4 are truly widows. ·If a widow has children or
grandchildren, they are to learn first of all to do
their duty to their own families and repay their
debt to their parents, because this is what pleases
5 God. ·But a woman who is really widowed and
left without anybody can give herself up to God
and consecrate all her days and nights to peti-
6 tions and prayer. ·The one who thinks only of
pleasure is already dead while she is still alive:
7 remind them of all this, too, so that their lives
8 may be blameless. ·Anyone who does not look
after his own relations, especially if they are
living with him, has rejected the faith and is
worse than an unbeliever.

9 Enrollment as a widow is permissible only for
a woman at least sixty years old who has had

¹⁰ only one husband. ·She must be a woman known
for her good works and for the way in which
she has brought up her children, shown hospitality to strangers and washed the saints' feet,
helped people who are in trouble and been ac-
¹¹ tive in all kinds of good work. ·Do not accept
young widows because if their natural desires get
stronger than their dedication to Christ, they want
¹² to marry again, ·and then people condemn them
for being unfaithful to their original promise.
¹³ Besides, they learn how to be idle and go around
from house to house; and then, not merely idle,
they learn to be gossips and meddlers in other
people's affairs, and to chatter when they would
¹⁴ be better keeping quiet. ·I think it is best for
young widows to marry again and have children
and a home to look after, and not give the en-
emy any chance to raise a scandal about them;
¹⁵ there are already some who have left us to fol-
¹⁶ low Satan. ·If a Christian woman has widowed
relatives, she should support them and not make
the Church bear the expense but enable it to support those who are genuinely widows.

✠

Paul begins this passage with instructions concerning
Timothy's attitudes toward various ages and sexes in
the community (with the typical Pastorals emphasis
upon propriety), but the mention of the honor he is to
show toward "true widows" (5:3) leads to a discussion
of this particular group (5:3–16).

In a social world constructed on a patriarchal basis,
widows and orphans were particularly vulnerable and
helpless. When the husband died, they were not only

bereft of support; they had nowhere to go. Widows had
two options: remarriage or destitution. For this reason,
the earliest legislation of Israel had shown special concern for widows and orphans. In no way were they to
be oppressed (Ex 22:21–24, Dt 24:17–18, 27:19),
and it was considered the obligation of others to help
them (Si 4:10, Jb 31:21, Ez 18:7, Is 1:16–20,
58:6–14). In Judaism, the support of widows, orphans
and other unfortunates became an organized community charity, for which alms were regularly collected
and dispersed. Acts 6:1, Jm 1:27, this passage, and
many others from documents written in the second century show us that in Christianity, too, the care of
widows and orphans was regarded as a community responsibility, and as a necessary corollary to authentic
faith (Jm 1:27, 1 Tm 5:8). Indeed, this passage indicates that something like an "order" of widows was
developing within the Church. Paul speaks of the qualifications for "enrollment" in this order (5:9). While
they are being supported by the community's resources,
these "true widows" devote themselves to prayer for
the community and to good works (5:5).

Paul clearly approves of this arrangement, but
expresses some hesitation on two points. First, he insists that the responsibility of providing for widows
rests not first of all with the Church as a whole, but
with families: "Anyone who does not look after his
own relations, especially if they are living with him, has
rejected the faith and is worse than an unbeliever"
(5:8). Nor is this responsibility only a man's: "If a
Christian woman has widowed relatives, she should
support them" (5:16). If families fulfill their obliga-

tions, then the Church will be able to support those
who are genuinely without other help (5:16).

Paul's other reservation concerns the enrollment of
young widows still of a marriageable age. He would
definitely prefer them to remarry (5:14). He is not
thinking here only of those "who think only of pleasure" and are dead even while alive (5:6), that is,
widows in name only who are out for a good time. He
is also afraid that the good name of the community
might be hurt (5:14) in the case of a younger woman
who is admitted to this special order of widows, and
then decides to marry again when "her natural desires
get stronger than her dedication to Christ" (5:11). She
will not have done wrong in this, but she will be condemned for having gone back on her promise (5:13).
And again, we see the sort of havoc being created by
the false teachers who find their favorite prey among
the women: "there are already some who have left us
to follow Satan" (that is, the false teachers, 5:15). As
we have seen repeatedly, Paul regards the natural
strength of the family as the best defense against the
encroachment of these seducers.

STUDY QUESTION: Does the Church today cultivate the
                same sense of ministry among those
                who are helpless and need its sup-
                port, as we find in Paul's discussion
                of widows?

1 Timothy 5:17 – 6:21
MONEY AND AUTHORITY

¹⁷ The elders who do their work well while they
are in charge are to be given double consideration, especially those who are assiduous in
¹⁸ preaching and teaching. ·As scripture says: You
must not muzzle an ox when it is treading out
the corn; and again: The worker deserves his pay.
¹⁹ Never accept any accusation brought against an
elder unless it is supported by two or three wit-
²⁰ nesses. ·If any of them are at fault, reprimand
²¹ them publicly, as a warning to the rest. ·Before
God, and before Jesus Christ and the angels he
has chosen, I put it to you as a duty to keep
these rules impartially and never to be influ-
²² enced by favoritism. ·Do not be too quick to lay
hands on any man, and never make yourself an
accomplice in anybody else's sin; keep yourself
pure.
²³ You should give up drinking only water and
have a little wine for the sake of your digestion
and the frequent bouts of illness that you have.
²⁴ The faults of some people are obvious long
before anyone makes any complaint about them,
while others have faults that are not discovered

²⁵ until afterward. ·In the same way, the good that
people do can be obvious; but even when it is
not, it cannot be hidden for ever.

¹ 6 All slaves "under the yoke" must have un-
qualified respect for their masters, so that the
name of God and our teaching are not brought
² into disrepute. ·Slaves whose masters are believers are not to think any the less of them because
they are brothers; on the contrary, they should
serve them all the better, since those who have
the benefit of their services are believers and
dear to God.

This is what you are to teach them to believe
³ and persuade them to do. ·Anyone who teaches
anything different, and does not keep to the
sound teaching which is that of our Lord Jesus
Christ, the doctrine which is in accordance with
⁴ true religion, ·is simply ignorant and must be full
of self-conceit—with a craze for questioning everything and arguing about words. All that can
come of this is jealousy, contention, abuse and
⁵ wicked mistrust of one another; ·and unending
disputes by people who are neither rational nor
informed and imagine that religion is a way of
⁶ making a profit. ·Religion, of course, does bring
large profits, but only to those who are content
⁷ with what they have. ·We brought nothing into
the world, and we can take nothing out of it;
⁸ but as long as we have food and clothing, let us
⁹ be content with that. ·People who long to be rich
are a prey to temptation; they get trapped into all
sorts of foolish and dangerous ambitions which
eventually plunge them into ruin and destruction.
¹⁰ "The love of money is the root of all evils" and
there are some who, pursuing it, have wandered
away from the faith, and so given their souls any
number of fatal wounds.
¹¹   But, as a man dedicated to God, you must

avoid all that. You must aim to be saintly and
religious, filled with faith and love, patient and
¹² gentle. ·Fight the good fight of the faith and win
for yourself the eternal life to which you were
called when you made your profession and spoke
up for the truth in front of many witnesses.
¹³ Now, before God the source of all life and
before Jesus Christ, who spoke up as a witness
for the truth in front of Pontius Pilate, I put to
¹⁴ you the duty ·of doing all that you have been
told, with no faults or failures, until the Appearing of our Lord Jesus Christ,

¹⁵   who at the due time will be revealed
       by God, the blessed and only Ruler of all,
       the King of kings and the Lord of lords,
¹⁶   who alone is immortal,
       whose home is in inaccessible light,
       whom no man has seen and no man is able to
          see:
       to him be honor and everlasting power. Amen.

¹⁷   Warn those who are rich in this world's goods
that they are not to look down on other people;
and not to set their hopes on money, which is
untrustworthy, but on God who, out of his
riches, gives us all that we need for our happi-
¹⁸ ness. ·Tell them that they are to do good, and
be rich in good works, to be generous and
¹⁹ willing to share—·this is the way they can save
up a good capital sum for the future if they want
to make sure of the only life that is real.
²⁰   My dear Timothy, take great care of all that
has been entrusted to you. Have nothing to do
with the pointless philosophical discussions and
antagonistic beliefs of the "knowledge" which
²¹ is not knowledge at all; ·by adopting this, some
have gone right away from the faith. Grace be
with you.

✠

There is a good bit of talk about money in this section of the letter. Paul has just discussed the support of
widows, and now addresses the issue of the support
owed its teachers and leaders by the Church
(5:17-18). The directive is clear enough: the Church
owes its leaders support, and double payment for those
who carry a double burden (5:17). This principle is
entirely consistent with Paul's view elsewhere on this
matter. Though he himself gave up the right to such
support, in order to be free of obligation to any one
community (except the Philippians; cf. Ph 4:15-18),
he insisted that it was a genuine right he sacrificed, not
a privilege (1 Co 9:3-18), and he supported this
stance by the same reference to Dt 25:4: "You must
not muzzle an ox when it is treading out the corn"
(5:18; cf. 1 Co 9:9). In addition to this saying of
Scripture, Paul here adds a saying of Jesus to the same
effect, "the worker deserves his pay" (cf. Lk 10:7).
Not only are the elders to be properly paid for their
efforts; they are not to be accused arbitrarily of wrong-
doing. Again, Paul cites the principle of Scripture
which was in general application: two or three
witnesses are required if any charge is to be seriously
considered (Dt 17:6; cf. 2 Co 13:1).

But if the community owes its leaders support, they
in turn owe the community hearts free from greed (cf.
3:4,9). Here is the basest motivation of the false
teachers, that they imagine that religion is a way of

making profit (6:7). Timothy and the teachers of the community are to understand that such greed spawns "foolish and dangerous ambitions" (6:9). Paul recalls the principle which was common in Hellenistic moral teaching, that "the love of money is the root of all evils" (6:10). It is a vice particularly reprehensible in the preacher, for the desire for gain corrupts the message of truth into flattery of those from whom payment is sought (1 Th 2:5) and results in "tampering with God's word" (2 Co 4:2). Compulsive desire for possession is a form of idolatry which denies the most evident fact about creatures: "We brought nothing into the world, and we can take nothing out of it" (6:7). The "profit" Paul sees coming from religion is a contentment with basic needs of food and clothing common to all humans (6:8), acceptance, that is, of life as it comes to us from God. The constant desire for more leads only to destruction (6:9).

The temptation to identify their worth with their money is especially strong for those "who are rich in this world's goods" (6:17). They, above all, need to be reminded that a hope placed in possessions is illusory. But if they place their trust in God, that is, if they recognize that life and worth come not from what they possess, but by what comes from God as gift, they will be able to share their material blessings with others, to "be rich in good works." Paul's words here are powerfully reminiscent of the sayings of Jesus on riches, especially in the Gospel of Luke 12:13–34. The rich are in no position to "look down on other people" (6:17), for they are as needful of the "only life that is real" (6:19) as all others, and this comes only by gift from God.

Paul's short exhortation concerning slaves in 6:1–2 is of special interest in this context, for it shows how the attitude of scorn can work from both ends of the social scale. For the first time in the New Testament, we find the explicit situation where both slave and master are Christian. Slaves who have learned from Paul that in Christ there is neither slave nor free (Ga 3:28, Col 3:11) may be eager to translate this principle into action, if not by actual rebellion, then by showing contempt for owners whose acceptance of the same principles has not led them to the release of their Christian slaves. But the freedom enunciated by Paul did not have to do first of all with social status. We have seen repeatedly that he was essentially conservative in his social ethics. There is paradox here, but not contradiction. "He who was called in the Lord as a slave is a freedman of the Lord. Likewise, he who was free when called is a slave of Christ" (1 Co 7:22). The breakdown of divisions brought about by Christ does not lead inevitably to the breakdown of the social fabric. But it relativizes the power structure of any societal arrangement by asserting that life and worth come not from where one is placed in the power structure, but where one stands before the Lord. Such a paradox makes intelligible the exhortation to slaves to serve their masters all the better, for they *too* are beloved by the Lord, and the picturing of this service as a kind of "lordly benevolence" shown by slave to master (the Greek word, *euergesia* behind the *JB*'s "have the benefit" (6:2), denotes the sort of liberality exercised by the powerful in the Hellenistic world).

As in 2 Tm 4:1–5, Paul concludes his instruction of Timothy with a solemn exhortation to fulfill worthily his call and profession, by fighting the good fight of the faith (6:12), and by avoiding the ways of the false teachers (6:11,20). Timothy is to continue to "speak up for the truth" (6:12), and can do this if he holds before him the example of "Jesus Christ, who spoke up as a witness for the truth in front of Pontius Pilate" (6:13). Paul has presented himself as a model for Timothy, but the ultimate model for the Christian teacher remains always Jesus.

STUDY QUESTIONS: Some have suggested that in the Pastoral Letters we find a "domesticated Paul." What is there in this last chapter which might support this description? Is such "domestication" a healthy development?

Titus
Letter to the Outpost

The short letter to Titus is remarkable in two respects. It is, first of all, difficult to place within Paul's career, such as we know it from Acts and his other letters. Acts 27:7 indicates that Paul touched down briefly in Crete, a large island of the Mediterranean south of Greece, during his perilous last trip to Rome as a captive. Nothing is said about his establishing a church there. Yet, Tt 1:5 states that Paul left Titus in Crete to "get everything organized there and appoint elders in every town." Titus' mission is a temporary one, for Paul plans to send Artemas or Tychicus (cf. Ac 20:4, Ep 6:21, Col 4:7, 2 Tm 4:12) as replacements, and expects Titus to join him in Nicopolis (there are several towns of this name) where he plans to spend the winter (3:12). Paul expects Titus to make travel arrangements for Zenas the lawyer (whom we know nothing of) and Apollos (whom we know as an associate of Paul; cf. Ac 18:24, 19:1, 1 Co 1:12, 16:12). There is no suggestion that Paul is in prison, and his mission appears to be in full swing. Titus fills in a space of Paul's career we did not know was blank.

The second remarkable thing about this letter is that although it covers much the same ground as 1 and 2 Timothy, it does so at quite a distinct gait. The situation appears rougher in every respect. The opponents are more aggressive, and are to be treated more aggressively (1:11, 3:10–11). Paul has harsh things to say about the character of the Cretans generally (1:12), and of the false teachers (here identified as Judaic, 1:10,14, 3:9), in particular. Furthermore, the instructions he gives Titus concerning the way people are to behave seem to suggest that these believers are not far removed from their former vices, and need remedial moral instruction of the simplest sort, as well as the Gospel message. The summaries of the Gospel in Titus correspondingly stress the "kindness and love of God our savior" (3:4) and the educative power of his grace (2:11–12). The New Testament document which most closely resembles Titus in these respects is 1 Peter, which was also written for newly converted pagans. From all indications, Titus' task was not an easy one.

Titus 1:1–16
THE ELDERS AND THE FALSE TEACHERS

¹ From Paul, servant of God, an apostle of Jesus Christ to bring those whom God has chosen to faith and to the knowledge of the truth that ² leads to true religion; ·and to give them the hope of the eternal life that was promised so long ago ³ by God. He does not lie ·and so, at the appointed time, he revealed his decision, and, by the command of God our savior, I have been commis-⁴ sioned to proclaim it. ·To Titus, true child of mine in the faith that we share, wishing you grace and peace from God the Father and from Christ Jesus our Savior.

⁵ The reason I left you behind in Crete was for you to get everything organized there and appoint elders in every town, in the way that I told you: ⁶ that is, each of them must be a man of irreproachable character; he must not have been married more than once, and his children must be believers and not uncontrollable or liable to be charged ⁷ with disorderly conduct. ·Since, as president, he will be God's representative, he must be irreproachable: never an arrogant or hot-tempered man, nor a heavy drinker or violent, nor out to

8 make money; ·but a man who is hospitable and
a friend of all that is good; sensible, moral, devout
9 and self-controlled; ·and he must have a firm
grasp of the unchanging message of the tradition,
so that he can be counted on for both expounding
the sound doctrine and refuting those who argue
against it.

10   And in fact you have there a great many people
who need to be disciplined, who talk nonsense
and try to make others believe it, particularly
11 among those of the Circumcision. ·They have got
to be silenced: men of this kind ruin whole families, by teaching things that they ought not to,
and doing it with the vile motive of making
12 money. ·It was one of themselves, one of their
own prophets, who said, "Cretans were never
anything but liars, dangerous animals and lazy":
13 and that is a true statement. So you will have to
be severe in correcting them, and make them
14 sound in the faith ·so that they stop taking notice
of Jewish myths and doing what they are told to
do by people who are no longer interested in the
truth.

15   To all who are pure themselves, everything is
pure; but to those who have been corrupted and
lack faith, nothing can be pure—the corruption is
both in their minds and in their consciences.
16 They claim to have knowledge of God but the
things they do are nothing but a denial of him;
they are outrageously rebellious and quite incap-
able of doing good.

☩

After an unusually full salutation, which, like the
greetings in Romans and Galatians, contains a brief

summary of the Gospel he has been appointed to preach (1:1–4), Paul turns at once to the matters at hand. Since Titus had been left in Crete to "appoint elders in every town" (1:5), Paul immediately sketches the qualifications for such leaders. As in 1 Tm 3:1, we find here an ambiguity in title, for in 1:7, without any warning or shift in subject, we find that it is the "bishop's" (*JB:* "president") qualifications which are being listed. Bishops and elders are apparently titles for the same office, here.

The list of virtues is much the same as in 1 Tm 3:1–7, with some noteworthy variations. First, it is somewhat remarkable that the bishop's children are not only to be believers, but "not uncontrollable or liable to be charged with disorderly conduct" (1:6)! The Gospel has not yet sunk deep roots. Second, the image of the bishop as manager of a household, which was suggested by 1 Tm 3, is here made explicit. The *JB* has "God's representative" in Tt 1:7 but the Greek has "God's household manager." Third, a couple of the virtues seem to point to an ambience of some harshness: the bishop is not to be "arrogant or hot-tempered." Fourth, the teaching function of the bishop suggested by 1 Tm 3:2 is here stated directly: the bishop is to have a firm grasp of the tradition, so he can teach healthy doctrine, on the one hand, and refute its opponents on the other (1:9).

This mention of the opponents leads Paul to a discussion of how they are to be dealt with. Apparently, these false teachers are Jews (1:10,14), who are causing considerable disruption ("ruining whole families," 1:11) by their aggressive and persuasive presentation of the Law, suggesting to these impressionable pagan converts that ritual purity is a requirement for Christianity (1:14–15). Paul dismisses them curtly. They claim to know God, he says, but their way of acting is a living denial of him (1:16). The Law they so guilefully peddle is but "Jewish myths and the commandments of men who are no longer interested in the truth." Christians have been made a "purified people" already by the saving work of Christ (2:14); for them, there is no longer "clean" and "unclean"; for those purified by the gift of God's own Spirit (3:5), "all is clean" (cf. Rm 14:20).

How can these hucksters proclaim a "purity," when they speak from minds and consciences which are thoroughly corrupted? Of course, to them, "Nothing can be pure" (1:15)! In his outrage, Paul pulls out all the rhetorical stops, even the quotation of "one of their own prophets" (the poet Epimenides of Crete, whose statement was well-circulated in the ancient world), to the effect that such troubles could be expected among the Cretans, for they were never anything but "liars, dangerous animals, and lazy" (1:12). Just this sharply is the bishop to rebuke the opponents: "They have got to be silenced" (1:11). And Titus should act the same: "You will have to be severe in correcting them, and make them sound in the faith" (1:13).

STUDY QUESTION: If a teacher or preacher today exhibited the qualities of the false teachers in the Pastorals, would he or she be recognized as a heretic, or welcomed as a revivalist?

GRACE AND GRACEFUL LIVING

¹ ² 2 It is for you, then, to preach the behavior which goes with healthy doctrine. ·The older men should be reserved, dignified, moderate, ³ sound in faith and love and constancy. ·Similarly, the older women should behave as though they were religious, with no scandalmongering and no habitual wine drinking—they are to be the ⁴ teachers of the right behavior ·and show the younger women how they should love their hus- ⁵ bands and love their children, ·how they are to be sensible and chaste, and how to work in their homes, and be gentle and do as their husbands tell them, so that the message of God is never ⁶ disgraced. ·In the same way, you have got to per- ⁷ suade the younger men to be moderate ·and in everything you do make yourself an example to them of working for good: when you are teach- ⁸ ing, be an example to them in your sincerity and earnestness ·and in keeping all that you say so wholesome that nobody can make objections to it; and then any opponent will be at a loss, with ⁹ no accusation to make against us. ·Tell the slaves that they are to be obedient to their masters and always do what they want without any argu- ¹⁰ ment; ·and there must be no petty thieving—they

must show complete honesty at all times, so that they are in every way a credit to the teaching of God our savior.

11 You see, God's grace has been revealed, and it has made salvation possible for the whole human
12 race ·and taught us that what we have to do is to give up everything that does not lead to God, and all our worldly ambitions; we must be self-restrained and live good and religious lives here
13 in this present world, ·while we are waiting in hope for the blessing which will come with the Appearing of the glory of our great God and
14 Savior Christ Jesus. ·He sacrificed himself for us in order to set us free from all wickedness and to purify a people so that it could be his very own and would have no ambition except to do good.
15 Now this is what you are to say, whether you are giving instruction or correcting errors; you can do so with full authority, and no one is to question it.

✠

The false teachers are upsetting whole households (1:11) with their propagation of the Law. Newly converted Gentiles, who but recently were "ignorant, disobedient, and misled and enslaved by different passions and luxuries . . . lived then in wickedness and ill-will, hating each other and hateful themselves" (3:3), had but little grasp of the moral behavior which was second nature to those who had grown up in Judaism and then became Christians. They were, therefore, easy prey for those claiming to offer a higher morality through observance of the Law and ritual purity. Not that the Greek world had not a standard of morality of great rigor and beauty espoused by its best philosophers; but the rude and raw people Titus had to deal with were not, apparently, heirs to that morality, either.

For the Gospel message to grow in such an environment, it was necessary to have some stability, and the new converts had to gain some sense of behavior consonant with the "healthy teaching" of the Gospel. For stability, Paul wants Titus to strengthen the family structure, by stressing the sort of good order that social arrangement depended on. Within this social structure, Paul wanted Titus to inculcate a life of virtue. In this passage, therefore, we find another version of the Hellenistic "household ethic," filled out with lists of virtues appropriate to each level within the household. There is little here which could not have come from a Hellenistic moral treatise. Few passages in Paul sound so thoroughly Greek as this one. We find ourselves within the shaping of the Gospel message to a distinctively Greek audience, one, moreover, which needed the most rudimentary instruction in morality.

In 2:11-14, Paul reminds Titus of the basis of Christian morality, the gift of God's grace. Paul sees these Gentiles as part of God's elect people (1:1), who have now received the "hope of eternal life that was promised so long ago by God, who does not lie" (1:2). Although they had been "ignorant" of God (3:3), and had lived lives filled with vice, "impiety and worldly ambitions" (2:12), the full dimensions of God's gift have been revealed (2:11) through the word of the Gospel (1:3): the salvation which comes from God is not intended only for the chosen people of the past, the Jews, but is being offered "to the whole human race" (2:11). The voice of the apostle to the Gentiles speaks here.

Paul summarizes in 2:14 the saving act of God in "Jesus Christ our savior." Jesus sacrificed himself on the cross in order to free humans from wickedness (there is a resonance of Ps 130:8, here), and to "purify a people so that it could be his very own" (cf. Ex 19:5). As in 1 P 2:9, the distinctive appellation of Israel as "God's People" is here applied without hesitation to a Gentile community.

And what does this grace of God lead to? A people which "would have no ambition except to do good." In the Greek, 2:14 says, "a people zealous for good works," but it is clear that Paul does not mean the works of the Law; rather, he means those manifestations of the virtuous life which he spells out in 2:12. For these immature Christians of Gentile origin, Paul stresses the educative power of God's grace: "It teaches us" how to give up that which does not lead to God, and how to live by the standard of morality appropriate to those "justified by his grace" (3:7). As in 1 and 2 Timothy, Paul expects the Christians of Crete to be able to look to Titus as the model of this way of life, both in what he teaches and in the way he lives (2:7).

STUDY QUESTIONS: How can the grace of God "teach us"? How is Paul's thought here related to his teaching on the transformation of our minds by the Spirit, in Col 3:10, Ep 4:23? Is the goal of grace moral behavior? Is the teaching of Titus in this respect a diminishment or enhancement of other Pauline teaching?

Titus 3:1–15
REBIRTH INTO LOVE

¹ 3 Remind them that it is their duty to be obedient to the officials and representatives of the government; to be ready to do good at every ² opportunity; ·not to go slandering other people or picking quarrels, but to be courteous and always polite to all kinds of people. ·Remember, there was a time when we too were ignorant, disobedient, and misled and enslaved by different passions and luxuries; we lived then in wickedness and ill-will, hating each other and hateful ourselves.

⁴ But when the kindness and love of God our ⁵ savior for mankind were revealed, ·it was not because he was concerned with any righteous actions we might have done ourselves; it was for no reason except his own compassion that he saved us, by means of the cleansing water of rebirth and by renewing us with the Holy Spirit ⁶ which he has so generously poured over us ⁷ through Jesus Christ our Savior. ·He did this so that we should be justified by his grace, to become heirs looking forward to inheriting eternal ⁸ life. ·This is doctrine that you can rely on.

I want you to be quite uncompromising in
teaching all this, so that those who now believe
in God may keep their minds constantly oc-
cupied in doing good works. All this is good, and
9 will do nothing but good to everybody. ·But
avoid pointless speculations, and those genealogies, and the quibbles and disputes about the
Law—these are useless and can do no good to
10 anyone. ·If a man disputes what you teach, then
after a first and a second warning, have no more
11 to do with him: ·you will know that any man of
that sort has already lapsed and condemned
himself as a sinner.

12   As soon as I have sent Artemas or Tychicus
to you, lose no time in joining me at Nicopolis,
13 where I have decided to spend the winter. ·See
to all the traveling arrangements for Zenas the
lawyer and Apollos, and make sure they have
14 everything they need. ·All our people are to
learn to occupy themselves in doing good works
for their practical needs as well, and not to be
entirely unproductive.

15   All those who are with me send their greetings.
Greetings to those who love us in the faith.
Grace be with you all.

✠

That the Cretans were in Paul's eyes a fairly unruly
lot is further indicated by this passage. In the instruction to be submissive to civil authority, Paul feels the
need to remind them that this submission should be an
expression of obedience, and not just the result of coer-
cion (3:1). They should be ready to cooperate in any
good work; they should stop "slandering other people

or picking quarrels," and instead "be courteous and always polite to all kinds of people" (3:2). We have the distinct impression that such equability would not come easily to this group, especially when we are reminded, in 3:3, of the misanthropic vices which characterized them before conversion. It is plain that such hostile folk as these would need an overwhelming gift of love if they were to learn to love themselves and others in a truly human fashion.

This gift of love, says Paul, has now come to them (3:4–7). In a tone of great tenderness, he reminds this refractory people of what has been given them. God has saved them, not because of anything they did or could do, but simply as an expression of his surpassing compassion (3:5), which has shown itself as "kindness and the love of mankind" (3:4). Their entrance into this saving love has been through baptism, which has given them a "rebirth" (cf. 1 P 1:3,23). Their old outlook and way of life has given way to something altogether new. Through baptism, they have received the Holy Spirit "which he has so generously poured over us" (3:6; cf. Rm 5:5), and which has the power of completely transforming them (3:5; cf. Rm 12:2, Ep 4:23, Col 3:10). By means of the free gift of God, they have been placed in an entirely new relationship with him: they have been made righteous (Rm 5:1, Ep 2:8), they have been made heirs (Rm 8:17, Ga 4:7, 1 P 1:4), whose hope is certain since it is based in God's love (3:7; cf. Rm 5:5, 1 P 1:3, Ep 1:18, Col 1:5). It is this gift of God's grace which "instructs" them how they should live, and which empowers them in so living. "This is doctrine that you can rely on" (3:8), for it is doctrine which leads to the same expression of "kindness and love of mankind" which God has shown first to us. The good works of those "who now believe in God" (3:8) are of help to other people, whereas quibbles and disputes about the Law are "useless and can do no good to anyone" (3:9). In 3:14, Paul indicates that the community is to learn to express its virtue in concretely helping others, especially in cases of urgent need (the *JB* translates this in a slightly different way).

The difficulty of Titus' mission is evident in this passage. He has, at one and the same time, to instruct the Cretan believers in the gentle virtues, and treat with severity those who oppose this teaching of love: "If a man disputes what you teach, then after a first and second warning, have no more to do with him" (3:10). If, in fact, Paul sent Artemas or Tychicus to replace him, Titus could not have been sad to leave.

STUDY QUESTION: The enduring puzzle of the Pastoral Letters is that, in passages such as this, thoroughly Pauline patches alternate with expressions and concerns not elsewhere found in Paul. What can account for this mixed nature of the Pastorals?

SUGGESTED FURTHER READING

COLOSSIANS:

1. F. O. Francis and W. A. Meeks, *Conflict at Colossae*, rev. ed. Sources for Biblical Study 4; Missoula: Scholars Press, 1975. For the advanced student, an invaluable collection of seminal articles on the Colossian heresy, the essay by Francis being particularly good.

2. R. P. Martin, *Colossians: The Church's Lord and the Christian's Liberty*. Exeter: Paternoster Press, 1972. A popular commentary, carried out with thoroughness and balance.

3. N. A. Dahl, "Christ, Creation and the Church," in *Jesus in the Memory of the Early Church*. Minneapolis: Augsburg, 1976. Pages 120–140. A scholarly article, written with Dahl's usual clarity and precision, this essay illuminates many features of Colossians and Ephesians.

Ephesians:

1. M. Barth, *Ephesians*. Anchor Bible, vols. 34 and 34A; Garden City: Doubleday & Co., 1974. A massive commentary which, throughout its detailed analyses, does not lose sight of the religious message. To be consulted rather than skimmed. Barth has an attractive popular book on themes of Ephesians: *The Broken Wall*, Philadelphia: Judson Press, 1959, which also can be read with profit.

2. C. L. Mitton, *Ephesians*. New Century Bible; London: Oliphants, 1976. Written from standpoint of non-Pauline authorship, this commentary is readable and, for its length, surprisingly thorough.

3. J. C. Kirby, *Ephesians: Baptism and Pentecost*. Montreal: McGill University Press, 1968. Provides a review of scholarship to date of publication, and approaches letter in its liturgical aspect.

4. H. Schlier, *Principalities and Powers in The New Testament*. New York: Herder and Herder, 1961. A scholarly study of the meaning of the angelic powers for the mystery of Christ and the Church, this work can be read by the serious student for insights into Colossians and Ephesians.

THE PASTORALS:

1. R. J. Karris, "The Background and Significance of the Polemic of the Pastoral Epistles," *Journal of Biblical Literature* 92 (1973) 549–564. A valuable collection of Hellenistic references pertinent to Paul's use of polemic. The present author has offered a refinement of Karris' position in "II Timothy and the Polemic against False Teachers: A Re-examination," *Journal of Religious Studies* 6–7 (1978–79), 1–26.

2. M. Dibelius and H. Conzelmann, *The Pastoral Epistles*. Philadelphia: Fortress Press, 1972. The classic scholarly commentary, rich in references to background materials.

3. J. N. D. Kelly, *A Commentary on the Pastoral Epistles*. New York: Harper and Row, 1963. A careful, concise and cogent reading of the letters for the general reader.

BIBLIOGRAPHY

1. R. ... ., "The Background and significance of the ... of the Pacific ... Railroad." ... Railroad History, no. ... (1972) 565-564. A valuable collection of ... pertinent to the ... ... policies. The revised edition also offered a ... on ... ... history and an ... ... A ... annual, Journal of Railroad Studies ... (1975-79)...

2. Wm. Z. Ripley and G. ... Combination, The Frequent ... Publications, ... useful commentary, rich in reference to background materials.

3. ... D. ... A Compilation of the Pacific ... ... New York: Harper and Row, 1969. A ... for ... ... and ... reading of the ... ... for the general reader.